TRANSFORMING EDUCATORS TO MENTORS

Sravya Ankem

© Sravya Ankem 2022

All rights reserved

All rights reserved by author. No part of this publication may be reproduced, stored in a retrieval system or transmitted in any form or by any means, electronic, mechanical, photocopying, recording or otherwise, without the prior permission of the author.

Although every precaution has been taken to verify the accuracy of the information contained herein, the author and publisher assume no responsibility for any errors or omissions. No liability is assumed for damages that may result from the use of information contained within.

First Published in March 2022

ISBN: 978-93-93388-65-0

BLUEROSE PUBLISHERS
www.bluerosepublishers.com
info@bluerosepublishers.com
+91 8882 898 898

Cover Design:
Geetika

Typographic Design:
Namrata Saini

Distributed by: BlueRose, Amazon, Flipkart

Preface

I started my teaching career after my post-graduation in electronics. I was appointed as physics faculty in the H&S department of a famous engineering college in Hyderabad. I was new to this platform and also was a fresher. But having good knowledge of the subject, and adaptability, I could deal with the learners of almost all branches of engineering in their first year. I started gaining confidence and learners were happy with the way I taught both practical and theory.

Later, I got an opportunity to work with Cambridge curriculum school (CAIE) in Hyderabad. I was given an opportunity to deal with CAIE, AS & A Levels for teaching Physics and Mechanics subjects. Though the subject was familiar, the teaching techniques, methodology, approach towards examinations, evaluation pattern, digital teaching, and working online were completely new.

I focused on all these new strategies by attending faculty development programs, enrichment, and evaluation programs both in online and offline mode organized by Cambridge Assessment International Education. Amidst my classes and professional development courses, I also used to watch teaching videos about various methodologies used in classroom teaching in various parts of the world, and why they are mostly followed by educators. Working and observing all energetic and vibrant educators around me, also helped me in the everyday learning process of classroom management, flipped class, including multiple intelligences in teaching, and more.

Blending all the learned techniques and implementing them in the teaching-learning process, I created my unique style of teaching. I succeeded in marking an impression in learners' minds. Moving ahead from a subject expert, I also was a mentor to many learners. The training I attended helped me to guide the learners who were in their adolescence; to face the challenges and overcome them with courage. Today, I work as a resource person and associate many training programmers for teachers and students at my venture 'Pioneers Academy'

With the experience in dealing with different levels of learners and various educators, I feel proud to have chosen to teach as my profession. Intending to share my learning which transformed me as a mentor, I started writing this book.

This book would be a handbook to the teaching community who wish to evolve as a mentor in the best possible ways competing with today's lightning-fast times.

It incorporates ideas for upgrading oneself from an educator to a mentor. It talks about the beautiful bond between an educator and a learner. It relates the teachings of eminent gurus during ancient India with present-day teachings.

An Educator's professionalism, reaction to situation, adaptation to new learning, self-introspection, nurture learners at different levels, raise standards to meet up the present day scenario by relating one class to real-life situations, incorporating creative and innovative ways of teaching, and many more are presented.

After sharing my experiences, through outreach efforts, I would be greatly privileged if at least one educator and one learner are benefited from my writing.

I would like to thank my mother for believing me as an efficient educator and also thank my brother and my husband for giving me valuable suggestions and helping me finish my writing.

I would like to thank Dr.M.Udaia Kumar, Founder of Reqelford International School, and Dr.Vidya Sravanthi Principal Reqelford International School for trusting me and allowing me to work in their prestigious organization.

I would like to extend my thanks to Mrs. Ssonu Ironi, Principal St.Peters School, Nacharam, Hyderabad, for her encouragement and for utilizing my services in the best possible way to reach out to the learners during my tenure.

I would like to especially thank Mrs.Rajitha Balasubramanyam, Vice-Principal CAIE, Reqelford International School, for being my role model and always guiding & encouraging me throughout my tenure. I admire her both personally and professionally.

Being an educator is nothing less than becoming a foster parent. I thought I would be helping, but through caring for them and nurturing them, I gained a lot. Thank you all my dear learners for your immense love. Thank you all parents of my learners for entrusting me and supporting me through thick and thin.

In the Memory of

MY NANNA

My Super Hero,
Tender in judgment,
Wise in counsel,
And Strong at all times.
I dedicate, with reverence, this simple book.

Dr. B.R. AMBEDKAR UNIVERSITY - SRIKAKULAM
Etcherla-532 410, Srikakulam, Andhra Pradesh, India

Prof. NIMMA VENKATA RAO
M.A (Edn); M.A.(Phil); Ph.D.
Vice-Chancellor

Phone : 08942-281422
Mobile : 9989739865

Date : 3.01.2022

Foreword

Education is the major driving force for socioeconomic transformation of the society. Globalization has brought about tremendous changes in all walks of life. The integration of the world economies poses a challenge to the teachers to acquire new skills required by today's society. Countries which have made significant investment in teacher training programmes have benefitted from globalization.

The challenge before us is to prepare our students as inventors rather than as job seekers. We have to prepare our students as real thinkers but not as routine followers. We have to prepare our students as planners but not as mere paper pushers. We have to prepare our students as innovators but not as imitators.

Today's world is all about re-inventing and enhancing oneself. Educators need to upgrade their skills in the technology driven age. The book "Transforming Educator to Mentors", depicts the changing roles of teachers from mere educators to mentors. The book is relevant and useful for teachers to upgrade their knowledge and information to aspiring teachers

The author Ms. Sravya Ankem has explained in detail the opportunity, commitment, and accountability of an educator in the society and the need for reinventing and enhancing oneself. The concept of comparing the educator's life to the life of the 'Kings of Skies – Eagle' is truly appreciable and valid. The book incorporates ideas for upgrading oneself from an educator to a mentor by enhancing the teaching learning process.

I appreciate the author's efforts and wish her success in all future endeavors.

(Prof. NIMMA VENKATA RAO)
Vice-Chancellor
Dr. B.R. Ambedkar University
SRIKAKULAM

Contents

Thankyou Educators' !!! 1
Teaching – "The Divine Art" 2
Spiritual Nature of Nurturing - Sadhguru 5
Teaching Humanity and Values 8
Iconic Teachers of India 11
Understanding and Enhancement of Self 17
Understanding Learners & Inclusive Learning 21
Adapt Yourself 27
Grasp the 'Essence of Teaching' 29
Kick start with a Successful Beginning 31
Essential Qualities for Fruitful Teaching 33
Be Professional 35
Success Mantra – An Educator's Daily Routine 39
Awareness & Involvement in Collaborative Work 42
Learning Domains — Bloom's Taxonomy 47
Learning Styles — Gardner's Theory of Multiple Intelligences 53
MI in Classroom 56
Multisensory Teaching-Learning 59
Classroom Discourses 61
Classroom Interaction 64

Classroom Questioning	66
Practical Approaches Involved in Teaching-Learning	71
Active Classroom vs Passive Classroom	75
Remembrance levels	77
Mind – Congenial Classroom	78
Flip Classroom	82
Thinking Skills	86
Importance of 'Planning for Instruction'	89
Classroom Management	94
Technology	97
Giving Feedback	100
Educators as Role Model	104
Educator as Leader	108
Educators as Nation Builders	112
Educator as Mentor	115
Importance of Professional Development for Educators	119
An Eye-Opener	122
Awards – Token of Appreciation	124
Why is Change Needed?	127
Bibliography	131

Thankyou Educators' !!!

For all that you do for learners in your classroom,

Making a million things happen for their benefit.

For keeping all your priorities on hold and making learner's day worthful.

For planning things ahead and focusing on learner's success.

For enhancing the plans that didn't work and needed little extra effort.

For all the smiles and accepting them as they are.

For encouraging & cherishing learners in their efforts,

and trusting them in their failure.

For upgrading and enhancing the methods in your teaching,

to reach the present generation of learners.

For being dedicated and honest to the promise you made as an educator.

You mean a lot,

You really mean a lot.

Teaching – "The Divine Art"

To the world, teaching is a profession. Some think it is just a cakewalk. Many say that anyone can teach if they have sound knowledge in a particular subject or topic. Some also say that it is just engaging learners with creative works. And many more critiques …

Educators come into the platform of teaching *'Not by chance but by choice*. Each one has its likeliness; some like working with little kids while some enjoy helping teens acquire knowledge. Every individual is a teacher at some point in their life. But, some continue their life journey in this platform enlightening young minds.

Educators are the creators. They have the power to influence people around them. Their responsibility towards mankind is exceedingly large. They have the scope to build a healthier society. Their influence impacts the lives of individuals. We usually find parents requesting the educator to talk in person with their child and advise them about some general thing (other than subject). They say 'my child will follow only your instructions'. Some learners express that their favorite subject is so and so, because of favoritism towards educators. Some teens open up their heartfelt personal issues and seek help from their trustworthy educators. There will be many examples like this in every educator's career. This is because of the impression we as educators create in those young hearts. They elevate us to be their role model.

Educators are good companions of the learners. They connect the classroom to real-life situations and make the session interesting. They cite everyday life examples and explain the topics that can be understood more thoroughly. This way of relating classroom teaching to real-life situations aids in the future of the learner.

Words of appreciation do wonders in the development of a learner. The challenging attitude is incorporated in the learner with these positive words by the educator. These words create a lot of impact in their later life while shaping their career.

Delivering the content is **teaching** while enabling the learner to experience and visualize the content being taught in his imaginary world is the **'Art of Teaching'**. The art of teaching transforms into divinity when the teaching and learning process allows learners towards goal setting and incorporating new knowledge, skills that add to a wide range of learning experiences.

Apart from delivering content, an educator needs to stand with the learner and encourage them, boosting with confidence which will sprout the trust within and thus meet success.

A passionate educator devotes to teaching life lessons as well. Acquiring knowledge and skill over a particular thing makes the person successful. But the success is valued and honored only by the personality. This personality has to be shaped and nurtured at a budding stage which is called childhood. However, some behaviors are hereditary which can't be changed, yet their impact can be reduced on the personality by incorporating various methods in the teaching-learning process. Learner blended with knowledge, wisdom, personality, and imbibed with values is called quality development.

The divinity in teaching evolves when an educator changes the scenario of life from the learner's perspective. What one becomes in life purely depends on the way one is educated. Analyzing the needs, essentials, organizing and prioritizing them are the most crucial things taught by an educator.

They help them by setting smart goals and mentoring them in self-evaluating and help them in developing problem-solving analysis. They channelize the flow of knowledge in the right direction to make one's future worthful.

Spiritual Nature of Nurturing -
Sadhguru

It is believed that in human life the age to get flourished or blossom is thirty-three years. If not channelized properly, this is the age to downfall as well. Let us understand this more clearly; the number thirty-three has a vital impact on one's career. All this happens naturally. And, it is also scientifically proven that – this age is like the trajectory which has its impact on the rest of life.

Attainment of eight and a half years of age is considered as childhood. Later the next twenty-four years are considered as a youth. Twenty-four years is equal to two pushkaras or two solar cycles. The sum of childhood and youth results in exactly thirty-two years seven months rounding to thirty-three years of age. By this time an individual should be able to channelize internal energy, inner geometry, and attain control over emotions. If one is prepared well with these positive energies from within, then their life would prosper in a very different way, which could be beyond expectations. Otherwise, it will start following the downhill path.

A child joins the school at two and half years and completes graduation at twenty-one years. This means learner spends most of their precious years of life with educators be it at school or college. So, we must incorporate methods of teaching that would work upon developing the inner mechanism of the learner. Including yoga, Dayana, physical and mental arts like martial arts, fine arts like painting, sculpture, and architecture, sports & games, and many others along with curriculum education is an advisable process. This should be done right from an early age so that it will benefit the learner channelize inner energy and thus develop a good character and personality. It also helps in being organized throughout their life and attains prosperity.

In this lightning-fast world, we need to work on personality, attitude, and communication skills more than educational qualifications. It is said that *"The doors of success are not opened by certificates but by you"*. It is in the hands of the educators to make education inclusive - leading to the great enhancement of life rather than making its conquest.

Education in India is worshipped. Education is believed as the third eye of an individual.it gives insight into all aspects of life. It raises the quality of thoughts and standards of living of an individual.

The Nature of Education is:

The very purpose of education is NOT only to earn money and to lead life happily, but its purpose is to enlighten one's mind, heart, and soul to lead a pious life.

Life without education is meaningless. It is not worth living life in ignorance. It is similar to the life of a beast in the jungle. Education raises the standards of living of an individual.

It is considered a lifelong process because every individual needs to learn new things at different phases to lead life hassle-free.

It enables individuals to adapt to an organized life through systematic institutions and regulations.

It develops the individual and thus the society. The development of society depends on its literacy percentage.

Individuals thinking, attitude, perspective mindset, and actions improve in their quality with the help of education.

It results in a constructive and socially desirable environment

Education is the power and treasure in the individuals which entitles man as supreme master.

Education is the holistic development of society and it brings prosperity and happiness to society. Therefore, its role in nation-building is significant.

Teaching Humanity and Values

Being Human doesn't mean that people possess humanity. Caring for others and helping others whoever is in need wherever and whenever possible is called humanity. It is the quality instilled in our minds and hearts from ages.

But in the present time, people are busy with their work and family pressures. The emergence of nuclear families, both parents working, single child and many more have declined the possibility to incorporate these habits in the young generations.

Being educators, we need to build this most prominent quality of being human and building values in our learners. This will further help them to build up their character and make them be a good citizen of the country.

Education in human values must be given prominence in all educational institutions for all age group learners as it is the only way to develop human society. Education should highlight the multifaceted development of human beings and the program of Education in Human values should be built around values like **faith, compassion, peace & harmony, conduct, and non-violence**.

The focus of value education should be more at the primary stage by incorporating value education classes which include moral stories, value-based skits, and theater arts, value-based drawings/poster making, practicing folk songs and dance, participation in scouts and guides further in National Cadet Corps (NCC), field trips, culture and heritage camps. Later in high school and senior secondary stages, the learners may have a choice to choose and take part in their place of their interest to extend their helping hands. In all the above-mentioned activities it is not only the school's interest but also the educator's role to encourage and initiate innovative methods of value education.

The Scheme of strengthening culture and values in education has been reformulated by NPE in 1986 and revised in 1992.

(a) Inculcation of values at pre-primary and primary stages in learners is highly recommended.

(b) Including value education as a part of the curriculum and conducting an assessment for the same makes the learners take it seriously

(c) Mainstreaming of cultural values into the educational system at all levels of education.

(d) Strengthening of in-service and pre-service training to educators including arts, crafts, music, dance, sports & games.

(e) Involving parent community for encouragement and strengthening of value system in learners.

Activities associated with value education:

- Use of audio-visual aids to enhance teaching-learning material.
- Conduct meetings, conferences, seminars for educators, parents, and learners to make them aware of the need to incorporate value-based education in the curriculum.
- Motivate learners to participate in meaningful creative activities aiming at inculcation of human values.
- Conducting Culture and Heritage exchange programs among learners at school and college levels.

- Case study and comparative study of values commonly inherited in all religions to be assigned for learners at senior levels.

- Documentation of strategies and experiences from innovative projects should be assigned to learners of senior levels.

- Research project in Education in Human Values must be encouraged to work on with.

A person with good values and ethics is a boon to society. Such a person, though working in any field such as politics, scientific & research field, defense, doctors, lawyers, etc. will surely work with a mindset to do something good for the society and mankind. And this quality is instilled in them at a very early stage of schooling and is nurtured by an educator at every level of learner's mental growth to shape them into the best citizen.

Iconic Teachers of India

Dronacharya and Parasurama

The ancient Hindu epic Mahabharata comprises two distinguished gurus. They personify teaching techniques in their way. Both gurus have trained their disciples to become great warriors, which decided the outcome of Mahabharata. While Parasurama mentored Bhishma, Dronacharya was the guru of both Pandavas & Kauravas.

Both these eminent gurus have imparted their wisdom and knowledge to their disciples equally, but Pandavas & Kauravas eventually fought on opposite sides.

By this act, it is evident that "Education is important, but what we choose to fight for with that knowledge is also equally significant". Though the education was alike; their moral compass would choose their final path of destiny.

Pandavas' education, right-mindedness, and wisdom led them to the path of victory.

Chanakya

Chanakya was a profound philosopher and jurist. He was also known as **Kautilya and Vishnugupta.** His reign was during the 4th century. He was the royal advisor in King Chandragupta Maurya's court.

His most significant writings Nitishastra (also called Chanakya Niti) and Arthashastra have an impact even today. His book Chanakya Niti contains numerous thought-provoking verses which are important in life.

His teachings reflect on "wisdom" as it mentions a lot of experiential realities from his time. He believes that "Wisdom is the key to lead a prosperous life"

Rabindra Nath Tagore

Tagore originates from Bengal. He is the **writer of the Indian national anthem 'Jana Gana Mana'** and also Srilankan National anthem. He is remembered for his scholastic excellence. He was an eminent teacher, a poet, a writer, and a freedom fighter who fought against the British government.

He believed that *"The main objective of teaching is not to give explanations, but to knock on the doors of the mind".*

He reinforced to use of activities for teaching which will help learners to develop both mental and physical abilities. His school at Shantiniketan, West Bengal emphasized teaching physical activities with basic education.

Savitribai Phule

She is renowned as India's first female teacher. Her sincere efforts towards female education make her deserve to be mentioned as one of the best teachers in Indian history. She along with her husband revolutionized British India and opened a school in 1848. She taught the untouchable. She always faced humiliations from the upper caste.

Finally, her endless effort was appreciated by the British Government. She raised her strong opinion against the atrocities committed on women especially on the women of lower caste.

Her fight towards 'girl child education was realized and the University of Pune is named after Savitribai Phule Pune University.

Swami Vivekananda

Swami Vivekananda was well known for his intellectual thoughts. He was special in discoursing known matters. He was the great Indian reformer.

He was the founder of 'Ramakrishna Mission' with a vision 'selfless service is the real worship of God in man', 'for one's liberation and the welfare of the world'.

His teachings involved spirituality and practical Vedanta. In the monastery founded by him, his followers were monks. They spread awareness about Vivekananda's teachings and serve the world in silence.

He emphasized the Gurukula system which was followed during the mythological age in ancient India. In this system, learners study and live together with educators.

Dr. Sarvepalli Radhakrishnan

The second President and the First Vice President of Independent India, Dr. Sarvepalli Radhakrishnan was a great teacher. He is one of the best teachers in Indian history. His birthday is celebrated as Teachers' Day in India every year fifth of September.

He imparted knowledge to his learners through his experiences. He gave prominence to spiritual education. His contribution to the field of philosophy was in understanding and sharing the most difficult concepts with his fellow teachers and learners.

He stands as an inspiration to present-day educators.

Dr. Sarvepalli Radhakrishnan believed that ***"A true teacher helps us think for ourselves".***

A.P.J. Abdul Kalam

Dr. A.P.J. Abdul Kalam is well known as a scientist to all of us. He was a scholar as well. He was also known as a missile man for his contribution to India's nuclear weapons and space engineering. With his writings and speeches, he inspired millions of children to move ahead in their lives. He was the 11th President of India.

Kalam was a great teacher who understood the level of students and used to think and respond to them from their perspective. He liked to spend quality time with learners.

He believed in 'practical educational thinking'. Kalam emphasized integrating conventional teaching methods into modern educational practices. One of his thought-provoking quotes is **"Some of the brightest minds in the country can be found on the last benches of the classroom"**.

Anand Kumar

Anand Kumar is an Indian Mathematics educator. He was born in Bihar, India, in 1973. He was graduated from Patna University. He was a gem in mathematics and bagged many awards for his brilliant brain. During his graduation, he had written papers on number theory, which was published in Mathematical Spectrum.

He served the underprivileged learners by providing them free coaching for JEE-Advanced and IITs entrance examination. This program was named **'Super30'** which is known to everyone as one of the best institutes having a good standard. Super30 was started in 2002 which works with a mission to help the needful learners with the best quality education. Records say that, by 2018. 422 out of 510 learners got the seat in IITs and JEEs.

- Anand Kumar was inducted in Limca Book of Records (2009) for providing education to underprivileged learners.
- His institute Super30 was included in the list of Best of Asia – 2010
- He was awarded the S.Ramanujan award for 2021 by IRDS
- Newsweek Magazine has included his school as the world's most innovative school.
- Bihar government awarded him with 'Moulana Abdul Kalam Azad Siksha Puraskar' in 2010.
- He was awarded by ABVP Bangalore with ' Prof.Yeshwanthrao Kelkar Yuva Puraskar- 2010'.
- In 2011 Europe's Magazine Focus has selected him as " one of the global personalities who can shape exceptionally talented people.
- He was respected with 'Rastriya Bal Kalyan Award' by the then president Ram Nath Kovind.
- In 2018 he was honored with Global Education Award
- He was felicitated in the US with the 'Education Excellence Award 2019' by FFE.

He marked his place in the education field and stood as an inspiration to all educators globally. He always trusted in 'As an educator – Knowing is not just enough, but, knowing the simplest way to impart the knowledge in learners mind is most important.

The iconic educators initiating from the mythological age to the modern age have a strong belief that along with basic education, learners should possess; wisdom, moral values, spiritual well-being, intellectual, spontaneity, valor or courage to travel in the path chosen, curiosity in new findings, experimenting, thought-provoking ideas, and creative, which are more significant for having a purposeful life.

This will be possible only by integrating conventional teaching methods with modern-day teaching practices. Now, it is time for us to think!!! Are we doing something to instill at least some of these qualities in our learners?

Understanding and Enhancement of Self

As an educator, the concept of **self** helps in gaining confidence and keeps us motivated throughout our teaching career. We need to understand and mound ourselves for the betterment of learners and thus society.

Self-enhancement is nothing but, developing a positive attitude towards self, which ripples the same while dealing with learners, balancing work–life, and thus promoting social development.

"The future belongs to those who believe in the beauty of their dreams"- **Elanor Roosevelt**

Self-introspection is a healthy way of understanding self and respecting oneself. A few things that have to be incorporated daily in one's life especially educators' lives are:

- Positive Affirmations
- Visualization
- Self – analysis
- Being optimistic
- Gift self a token of appreciation

As we all are educators, let us revisit Erik Erickson-stages of personal development in Psychosocial Development.

According to Erik Erickson stages of personal development involve eight steps;

STEP 1: Trust vs. Mistrust (birth – 18 months)

This is the age where the infant will develop basic trust especially towards the mother's love, and who fulfills hunger.

STEP 2: Autonomy vs. Shame or Doubt (18 months– 3 years)

This is the age where a child starts trying not to be dependent as he learns to walk, sit, move, hold things.

STEP 3: Initiative vs. Guilt (3-6 years)

At this age, the child joins the school and tries to learn by observation, imitation. He develops motor skills, language skills, and develops curiosity towards exploring things. The child believes in "what he dreams of he would be that."

STEP 4: Industry vs. Inferior (6-13 years)

The child learns new things. Success and failure are experienced by a child at this age. Success boosts up confidence while failure creates a negative impact which may hinder future learning abilities.

STEP 5: Identity vs. Role confusion (13-21 years)

At this age friends group, importance dominates the authority coming from parents. The child tries to establish self-identity. Reassembly of basic ego, the way he is brought up, and varied opportunities available display a role of confusion.

STEP 6: Intimacy vs. Isolation (21-39 years)

This age is called young adulthood. A new relationship of trust and intimacy establish with other individuals.

STEP 7: Generatively vs. Self-absorption (40-65years)

This is the age people involve in developing an interest in training and guiding the next generation. This is the age they need to grow otherwise they become stagnate and lose themselves in self-absorption.

STEP 8: integrity vs. Despair (65 years and above)

In late adulthood, an individual lives in the memories of their past. Some memories bring realization while some end in despair.

As per Erikson, every individual undergoes these eight stages of development. Being an educator, be it for pre-primary, primary, secondary, or higher secondary, it is our primary duty to take charge of the learner's overall development i.e from age 3 to 21 years as the learner spends most of the valuable years of life in schools and colleges.

To take up this responsibility in an effective way, first, let us perform an exercise on a self-analysis by answering the below.

1. Describe your pre-primary/primary/secondary/higher secondary years in school.
2. What new things have you learned during those years?
3. How did you relate yourself to your peer group?
4. What was your feeling when you interacted with new peers/relatives?
5. How successful were you while resolving problems that you encountered?
6. What was the influence of your educators in your schooling? (as per STEP 3,4,5)
7. Analyze the above i-vi and describe what kind of an educator **you want to be**?

Your description of **'what kind of an educator you want to be'** would help you move on the righteous path and enhance your **'self'** to blossom as a mentor. Your experiences as a learner will pave a path to make you a successful educator.

Understanding Learners & Inclusive Learning

Having diverse styles of learning, learners have a varied pace of learning. As the educator interacts with all learners of the class daily, they should be able to identify learner's style and their pace of learning. An educator should plan interesting and creative teaching practices to encourage each learner of the class to learn and gain knowledge equally.

As learners come from different backgrounds and cultures, the educator has to take initiative to know more and understand their learners. This will help educators to adapt diverse skills, attitudes, techniques to impart knowledge in the classroom and thus making the teaching-learning process successful. Educators must be impartial and accept all types of learners in their classes.

Gifted Learners

Learners with high intellect and outstanding creativity are known as gifted learners. They are independent & quick learners with good organizing skills. Educators dealing with gifted learners need to be sound in subject knowledge, very informative, and utmost creativity to meet the expectations of this group.

Some instructional strategies that help educators deal with gifted learners are mentioned below:

- Be ready for out of box questions
- Provide them with open-ended questions and activities

- Allow them to select and work on self-initiated projects
- Make divergent as a part of classroom questioning
- Assign leadership roles to enhance their management skills

Slow Learners

A slow learner is a child who has average intelligence levels. He has difficulty in learning subjects and is called a struggling learner. But slow learners may have interest and may excel in other co-curricular activities like sports, music, dance, playing instruments, robotics, and painting. The interest of such learners needs to be identified and encouraged by both educators and parents.

But, as we know the importance of education, a few strategies need to be followed to attract and teach this set of learners:

- Inculcate interest in the topic/subject by incorporating any one of the learning styles (audio-visual, bodily-kinesthetic, musical, etc.) that best suits the classroom
- Care has to be taken that no educator or learner will label the slow learners or criticize them. This will lower their confidence.
- To grasp and understand a concept, slow learners require more time and more repetitions. The educator needs to be patient and try to repeat the concept to make them understand.
- The educator needs to understand that they need little more help and do not require a special education school as they have their medical records normal.
- They may have difficulty in social interaction. This may be not only due to lesser mental ability but maybe because of poor health, social and economic background.

- Treating them with no difference and yet encouraging and boosting confidence in them to flourish is very important to both educators and parents

Disabilities

The child who is not able to comprehend a particular thing is called disability. Disability does not mean the learner has a low IQ or is mentally retarded. They have issues in understanding a few aspects of math concepts, reading skills, and more. The disabilities may have occurred because of hereditary, over usage of drugs in pregnancy.

Some learners can overcome their disability if proper support, guidance, and encouragement are given. But it takes more time to overcome Few disabilities are difficult to overcome. But, the learner can learn and complete schooling with these disabilities as well. It is the educator who has to adapt various techniques while such learners exist in the classroom. These set of learners do not require special education schools

Dyslexia – This is referred to as a reading disorder. The learner may have difficulty in the identification of letters and reading the word in reverse. This is observed in primary schooling. With consistent effort and effective teaching techniques, one can overcome it.

Dysgraphia – This is referred to as a writing disorder. Learners may be good at oral answering but, writing is difficult for them. They say something and write the wrong spelling. Regular monitoring and practice will help the learner to overcome this disorder.

Dyscalculia – Learners having difficulty in understanding math concepts or solving mathematical operations is called dyscalculia. If not taken care of in the early stages, the learner may not show interest in the subject. The educator must take initiative and incorporate activities, use the math lab for a detailed explanation.

Dystopia – Learner feels depressed and does not want to interact with peers or educators. Such learners may have family issues, social issues, and more. They must be guided to visit the school counselor who has various methods to help.

Dysmorphia – Learners having issues with the shape of their body or a part of their body is referred to as dysmorphia. They may have difficulty in walking, standing, or writing. Such learners must be given a helping hand and be treated equally with other learners.

Aphasia – learners having an oral disorder like stammering come under the aphasia category. Regular reading sessions may help them to overcome as they grow older. Educators must be vigilant that bullying does not happen to such learners.

Dyspraxia – Having an issue with coordination in body parts is called dyspraxia. These learners will not be able to perform kinesthetic skills properly.

ADHD – Attention deficit hyperactivity disorder is a disorder in which the learner has less attention towards the task given and is hyperactive also. These kids use gestures, repeated action behavior instead of talking. This is generally seen in kids below four years. If observed at a later age also, then necessary care has to be taken.

Autism spectrum disorder – Issues related to cognitive and emotions are called autism spectrum disorder. These learners are not social. They have problem-solving problems, speaking, interacting with others. They need to be guided to visit the school counselor for help.

Classrooms are a combination of gifted, slow learners and learners with disabilities. Such kind of classroom is referred to as inclusive classrooms. The educator must be positive towards all types of learners in the class. Activities need to be planned in such a way that it will not be boring to gifted learners or make it impossible for learners with disabilities to participate in them.

A well-planned educator only can effectively make the teaching-learning process successful in such inclusive classrooms. Educators must communicate with parents of learners (with disabilities) and discuss the best possible ways to help their kids in the classroom.

Ways to Create an Inclusive Classroom

An inclusive learning environment addresses inequities in the classroom and improves learners' retention. Inclusion is the degree to which all learners in a community are **welcomed, valued, respected, heard, and able to participate equally**. Educators must realize that learners are diverse and adapt varied learning styles. They require different supports to improve their chances of success.

Tips for creating an Inclusive Environment in the classroom:

Explore bias and assumptions

- Educators need to understand that their own experiences are probably different from their learner's. They may probably even differ from co-educators. They should give chance to learners to express themselves.

- Inclusive educators must acknowledge their learners' abilities, beliefs, background, sexual orientation, economic status shape their learning and reflect on their responses.

- Educators shouldn't make assumptions about their learners about 'who they are?' and 'How they learn?' instead they need to allow learners' experiences to shape the classroom.

Build a relationship with learners

- Learning more about students' personal learning experiences and challenges can help us understand the barriers they face in our classroom.
- To build a healthy relationship with learners', the educator needs to use learners' names during the classroom activities or teaching.
- Educators need to take time to examine the curriculum. There are different ways to know about the curriculum; authors, speakers, mentors, case studies, examples, learning styles.

Adapt instruction to the individual needs of learners

- Planning to have a collaborative and communicative class that supports all learners is of utmost priority. It sometimes brings special education into regular classroom
- Educators need to open up and ask learners their preferences in learning and consider them in planning a lesson or an activity in the classroom.
- When learners see that their own experiences are reflected in the classroom, they can connect better and increase their chances of success.

Co-Plan and Co-Teach

- Discussions with experts and colleagues for ideas will help in executing a better inclusive classroom.
- Valuable information may be acquired while discussions with experts and colleagues happen, as they share their experiences.

Creating an inclusive classroom is a continuous process.

Educators may start it right from where they are today!

Adapt Yourself

Adaptation; is the ability to accept change around us and move on with very less or no issues. Every one of us experiences novelty in many situations of our life. Some of them include; starting a new business, transferring to a new city, moving abroad for further studies, the first day of school. To what maximum extents are we able to accommodate these new situations is adaptability.

For an educator, adaptation is required while interacting with new students and their parents, discussion with new colleagues, unpredictable situations in classroom or laboratory, the unexpected change in timetable, uninformed stay back duties.

Other things apart, being adaptive in the classroom enhances educators' well-being. It also helps to prevail a healthy learning atmosphere. This expects a positive attitude, pleasantness, understanding, and response to the situation with less involvement of emotions like frustration or mood swings.

As our family life, so is our work-life – full of uncertainties. We as educators need to be challenging and ready to accept them. We need to integrate new knowledge with a blend of technology to meet up the expectations of the present-day teaching-learning process.

These situations prepare educators to adapt to successfully navigate them. Adapting involves adjusting lesson pacing to better engage students, lowering tension when a topic is not happening as per the scheduled lesson plan, indulging in collaborative work with new colleagues. Adaptability is something educators must inherit regularly which in turn plays a vital role in helping them achieves their goal.

Supporting adaptability practice in educators

Adaptability may be considered as one factor in supporting educators' well-being and promoting teacher retention.

Ideas for supporting adaptability in the practice

- Inviting educators' input in decision making,
- Providing educators with choices in curriculum and policy development,
- listening to educators' perspectives,
- Expressing confidence in educators' abilities
- Word of appreciation

The above-mentioned practices provoke a sense of empowerment and belongingness in the workplace. Together, these approaches may also help educators to be more adaptable at work.

Grasp the 'Essence of Teaching'

This is a story about an educator who set an example of an **'educator'**.

Mr.Bhaskaran is a successful businessman who runs a textile company. He is usually busy with board meetings, abroad trips for business expansion. He occasionally pays a visit to his hometown and spends time with his parents, childhood friends rejuvenates, and gets back to work.

In his recent visit, he met his school teacher who taught him math in grade nine. On his way home, as he saw his teacher walking down the street, with due respect Mr.Bhaskaran invited his teacher to visit his house for some coffee. And the teacher had no reason to say 'NO' to Mr.Bhaskaran's invitation.

Seated on the balcony and having a cup of coffee viewing at the dusking sun, their conversation started. It was very formal talk in the beginning, but later they flew with their throwback memories.

Suddenly Mr. Bhaskaran thanked his teacher saying 'Thank you, Sir, for being so kind on that day. The teacher asked innocently 'about which day are you talking?' then Bhaskaran recalled the incident – 'In my ninth standard one of my friends brought a costly watch to the class. It was so attractive that I felt it would be mine. During the lunch hour, I picked the watch from his bag and hid it in my pocket. As soon as he realized that the watch was missing, he complained about the issue to you as you were our class teacher'.

'Then you asked the class politely about the issue and assured us that there would be no punishment if the watch was returned voluntarily. As none of us responded, you asked us to close our eyes and stand in our place. You came searching for it for each one of us. And you found it in my pocket. You returned it to my friend. But, you have never called me to talk about the issue. That day was an eye-opener to me. I felt shameful and thought to apologize for my deed, but I couldn't dare to approach you. The lesson I learned that day is the result of what I am today. Saying these words Bhaskaran's eyes rolled in tears. He apologized to his teacher's heart fully for all that had happened.

The teacher stood up, smiled gently adjusting his spectacles, and asked in a low voice "Was that you"? He then said, 'that day as you all closed your eyes, I did close my eyes too. I was afraid! I might not have the same impression on the child as earlier if I knew him. I never knew until you revealed it now. Listening to this Bhaskaran was speechless and was proud to be a learner of such a great teacher.

Time for self-analysis!!!

1. Your reflections on Mr.Bhaskaran's story.
2. Assume that the same situation as in the story happened in your class and was brought to your notice. How would you handle it?

Be genuine with your answers for a perfect transformation in you.

Kick start with a Successful Beginning

Your zest is the reason for you to be on this 'education platform'. Focus on your belief and kick start with a successful beginning. It may be years of experience you have acquired in teaching, but every academic session is a new beginning. And, we need to kick start with a successful beginning to see the end to be successful.

Dream — Dream big - dream very big. We should always have big dreams and chase them with courage and determination. There's a famous quote *"If you can dream it, you can do it. Aim at the moon! You will at least land in stars"*.

As an educator, our dream (about learners) may be having a successful academic year, receiving the best teacher award for the year, cent percent pass in my subject, at least five of my subject students should score 100/100.

1. Visualize

"When you visualize, you materialize"- Denis Waitley

Visualization is the greatest gift for mankind. Some say it is daydreaming. Yes, it is daydreaming but with an urge to make it real.

As an educator, we need to visualize our dreams that it has turned out true. Only then, you can make a difference. Not to be one among the flow you should visualize your dreams.

2. Prioritize and Plan

First things' first……Planning plays a crucial role for an academic session to take place in an organized and systematic way.

3. Take Action

Dreams don't work until you take action. The only way to make your dreams come true is to live them. As your dreams are big, your preparedness to handle them should be tough enough. The result of your efforts will be seen in the learners' progress.

4. Face Hurdles

A journey without hurdles is not considered a perfect journey. As we all know - 'No pain no gain'. Hurdles are the **challenges** we come across in our journey. They put us on the right path if we are deviating.

5. Re-Organize the Plan

Finding a solution to the challenges teaches the educator how to deal with the learner appropriately. So we need to work on re-organizing our action plan.

6. Celebrate the success

Success is the result of visualization of a big dream, dedication in planning it, learning from challenges, and persistence. Thus achieved a dream is wonderful.

Every educator who has worked through thick and thin for their learners will feel the celebration of success at the end of the academic session.

Essential Qualities for Fruitful Teaching

An Educator should possess some unique characteristics which make the teaching-learning process purposeful. These essential qualities imbibed in the personality of an educator make the difference in their teaching styles. Some qualities may be dominant and some may be submissive but an educator possesses all these features.

Open-minded

An educator is always a learner by **self**. The willingness to try new things, or to listen, understand and consider others' ideas if they make sense in that situation is open-mindedness. This quality invites various inputs from colleagues, which would be helpful. This does not mean that we as an educator, have no ideas or we are indecisive. Yes, we do have ideas, but open-mindedness gives us scope to use our wisdom to choose the best fit solution.

Independent

The educator is the king of the classroom. To the learners, the educator is their hero. There lies an inseparable bond between the learner and educator. As the educator knows their learner's acceptance, they should be independent in taking decisions about; dealing with the lesson plan, teaching, and assessment methods. This independence helps in incorporating many new ways educator dreams of teaching, resulting in a purposeful session.

Creative

Creative educators customize their learning activities and also adapt techniques and strategies from their peers to make their class more informative and effective. Creativity is the way we present a regular thing differently. We can incorporate videos, PPT's, models, charts, role-plays in our teaching.

Optimistic

The educator who has hope and confidence in their learners is optimistic. This quality of an educator always boosts up confidence and fills in positivity, so that they start believing in themselves. This impact will be evident in the slow learners.

Emotionally strong

According to psychologist Paul Eckman, human life is filled with emotions. He suggested in the 1970s which was universally experienced in all cultures. The six emotions given by him are; happiness, sadness, disgust, fear, surprise, and anger.

It is a well-known fact that these emotions have a huge impact on one's life. The most important quality of an educator is NOT to carry negative emotions to class. This may be an obstructer to having a healthy classroom environment. The educator should be emotionally strong that whatever might be the situation, the harmony of the class is maintained.

Characteristics are inbuilt. Some are hereditary as well. But, to adapt some good qualities, is essential in the platform we stand on. Being the creators of society, we need to modify a few things in ourselves, thus making our teaching fruitful and also the society a healthy place to learn and gain knowledge.

Be Professional

Sound in subject knowledge

There is no scope for manipulation in teaching. Today's learners are smart enough to test the knowledge of educators. They are equipped with all the required gadgets, which make it possible for them to reach the world with a single click. But as competent educators, we need to prove that these gadgets cannot replace our teaching. This is possible only when an educator is a genius in the subject. Along with subject knowledge, we need to keep updating ourselves timely with technology as well.

Professional appearance

Language proficiency

Globally, the English language is used for communication (almost 90 percent). To expose us at that level we need to acquire English language proficiency. We need to respect our local languages but at the same time, we need to develop other language proficiency.

We all know that language is mostly learned by speaking, reading, and listening. A word listened to 21 times registers in our subconscious memory and reflects in our vocabulary unknowingly. Competent educators make add on these in their routine and make their learners also follow it.

Decorum

Across the world, educators have a great admiration when compared with other professions. The teaching profession is a highly respected platform. A competent educator has always maintained decorum, propriety, and etiquette.

Accountable

The honesty and sincerity towards our work is the measure of our commitment to it. Teaching needs that commitment. A committed educator is always accountable to their learners. Parents and management fall in the next place.

Our accountability towards them in all aspects will result in their bright career.

Time management

Time is the most valuable asset in this universe. Some things may be brought back with effort, hard work, dedication, pain, or guilt. But, not even a second passed by can be brought back. Such a valuable asset must be acknowledged by all of us.

The competent educator can instill this in the minds of their learners by just following it by themselves. Time management not only insists on being on time, but it is also about being punctual in the completion of works and on-time submissions.

Belongingness

The magical bond that happens between an educator and a learner is a miracle. Learners trust us as their well-wishers and express their feelings be it a class teacher or subject teacher. Similarly, the educators receive the good and mischief of the learner and nurture them with utmost care and concern in the righteous path as their child.

Education should not be about molding learners the way we want, but about supporting their natural longing to know and blossom.

Collaborative work

Collaborative work is recommended in all fields. Educators do follow this way of working. In collaborative work, we share ideas and work together to reach a common goal. As competent educators' our common goal is the learner's achievement. All subject experts of a class need to have a discussion and work together in achieving success. Teams educate and learn from each other. It improves mental health.

We need to make ourselves flexible to work in teams with peace and harmony.

Growing by betterment

A competent educator always grabs the opportunity to participate in the faculty development program, teacher enrichment program, induction program, workshops, and seminars. On these platforms, many experienced people share their ideas and views. We get a lot to learn from them. While taking part in such programs, we evolve and make a better version of ourselves.

Creative

A competent educator needs to showcase oneself differently. The ability to mark your way of teaching is a creative educator. A creative educator incorporates various innovative ways to make the learner understand the concept. Including games, quizzes, drawings, puzzles, debates… along lecture method will make a big difference in teaching. Here, Gardener's multiple intelligence theory may be taken into consideration.

Create your style…. Let it be unique for yourself and yet identifiable for others!!!

Professional conduct

A competent educator understands teaching as a responsible profession. And, maintains the standards of professional conduct and provides leadership to improve learners' overall development and well-being.

Introspection

A professional educator must introspect considering all the learners in the class gain knowledge of his / her teaching equally. A variety of assessments will be conducted and feedback will be taken. On the results of these assessments, educator learns to make necessary amendments in the teaching-learning process.

This process should take place more often to gain good results. It also helps the educator reach year-end goals with less effort.

Success Mantra – An Educator's Daily Routine

Preparedness

A well prepared class gives the satisfaction of a delicious meal !!!

Apart from teaching, we also have the responsibility of our family. In this busy schedule, sometimes it may not be possible to get prepared for the class. For such situations always have a PLAN B ready. It can be a surprise test, revisit of any topic, conducting; debate, quiz, pep talk. But never teach a new in unprepared class.

(Make sure this situation does not repeat very often)

Compete

The best competitor you have is YOU. Compete with yourself and be the best version of yourself. Organize, take time for preparation, begin with an open mind and work towards your dream.

Think win-win

We look for alternatives that allow everyone to win. We think win-win is a situation where we have to face the conflict between mind and heart. But win-win is a situation where everyone wins because educators work in collaboration, not individually. So a satisfying decision agreed by all ascends towards the action plan. Win-win comes from character traits of integrity, maturity, and mental ability.

Observe and Act

We learn a lot from observation and listening. It can also be considered a skill that every individual should develop. To understand a person deeply, one should listen to what they say without interrupting them. Listening connects us with a person intellectually and emotionally. It enables us to understand their inner feelings.

Now, time to take appropriate actions. Upon the considerations of your listening, create understanding which is seeking to be understood.

Sharpen yourself

We sometimes feel exhausted and bored managing the work-life cycle. This is the time we need a break. It does not mean we need to visit a tourist spot. We can just take a day off and stay home, take a rest, rejuvenate, and bounce back to work. This break is very much needed to retain the best in you. This helps in 'Enhancement of self'.

A balanced program for self is required for every individual. It includes aspects like;

- **Physical**

Involving yourself in having a wholesome diet and physical activity like exercise, walking, and aerobics improves **physical fitness**. A healthy body symbolizes active participation in daily activities, creates good vibes in the workplace and

- **Mental**

Reading, writing, and thinking help in stabilizing **mental wellness**.

- **Emotional**

Yoga and meditation help **conquer the self**. It defines our inner thoughts.

- **Spiritual**

Spending time in spiritual activities, performing rituals, being close to nature helps in gaining **calmness to the mind**.

- **Social**

Being social animals, we need to **maintain healthy relationships** with family and friends.

Awareness & Involvement in Collaborative Work

The educator should understand the learning style and levels of thinking of their learners. It is evident in many types of research that, productive teamwork helps to gain knowledge about the learning styles of learners. It has the power to change the culture of schools and make continuous learning possible in a very efficient pattern.

Collaborative work is not possible overnight. It involves understanding the colleagues by observation, having patience, and persistence. And, over a period of time educators in a team will learn what makes their teamwork effective and ways that they contribute to the goals of the school and are capable of being sustained.

For learners to achieve comprehensive and all-around development, working in teams is important in various dimensions. Collaboration is not only important among educators, it is also important among the learners, and between educators & parents as well.

Collaborative work among the learners has numerous benefits. A few of them are discussed below:

- **Improvement of Social Skill**

In group work/collaborative work, learners help each other and work together for the benefit of their group. They participate actively, encourage one other, listen to each other's ideas, criticize constructively and make the best outcome possible. In this process, they make friends, overcome shyness and talk to others, improve language skills and vocabulary, resolve conflicts, enhance thinking skills. Educators must ensure to incorporate group projects and activities which make the learning along with enhancing social skills.

- **Build Confidence**

It should be accepted that every individual learner is benefited personally from teamwork. Every contribution to the project makes the learner feel valued which in turn boosts confidence in them. This will be the platform where the learners can showcase their talent. Because, completion of the project not only involves subject knowledge, it also requires fieldwork, technology, presentation skills.

- **Enable Peer Learning**

Educators must be vigilant while making groups for a project. The group must include gifted, average, and slow learners equally in it. This will solve the purpose of sharing ideas and enriching knowledge amongst the learners. As completion of a project requires different aspects, each learner has the scope to exhibit their area of talent while other learners of the group learn it. An effective team will share all the responsibilities equally and gather more information which is effective than a worksheet done individually.

- **Sharing Ideas**

Educators always have the right to interfere informally to check the status and progress of the project. They can help the learners in enhancing the outcome of the project by sharing a few ideas and improvising a few instructions. Such interactions can take place in staff rooms. Educators must also ensure the boundary of offering advice. However, sharing ideas amongst the group will take place.

- **Classroom Environment**

Classwork becomes more rewarding and enjoyable with group activities. Learners welcome the change of collaborative tasks in their daily routine. The educator must ensure a few things strictly: the rubric to be discussed thoroughly, be wise in the grouping, assign duties and specify submission deadline.

- **Effective school**

Learners' achievement and well-being are not only influenced by the teaching practices of individual educators, but also by the school environment and culture. Incorporating collaborative work in the teaching-learning process makes the school successful and innovative. Successful schools always follow best practices.

Collaborative work among Educators has numerous benefits. A few of them are discussed below:

Teamwork among the educators is a sign of the successful functioning of the organization. It displays harmony, focus, and dedication of the team towards a common goal. It also creates a splendid learning environment for its learners.

- **Resolving Issues**

When collaborative work possesses among the educators, issues are addressed to a greater diversity of knowledge. The skills and experience of different educators resolve the issue by pooling expertise. It gives an opportunity to learn problem-solving techniques from each other.

- **Strength**

The strength of the team depends on trust, the professional relationship amongst educators, and also between educators and higher authorities (like coordinator, HM, Principal). An efficient team works productively and gives out faster outputs. Working as a team reduces the workload through sharing good practice, sharing worksheets, activity cards, save time in preparation of TLM, charts. The team gains good results than individual work as sharing and caring takes place.

- **Meet-up**

The members of the team should meet up at least once a week to discuss the progress of work. This meet-up is important to enable the team to discuss new ideas & plans, prioritize and accomplish tasks that will benefit learners eventually. Department meetings, staff meetings, team/group (educators about a class) meetings are essential to be held frequently. This benefits the educators to communicate and maintain a healthy professional relationship.

- **Benefit to Learners**

Members of the team can discuss constructively regarding learners such as behavioral problems, signs of other problems, lack of concentration, lack of understanding of a particular learner of the class and find ways to help them in the best possible way. Educators must make sure that the learners are not labeled with their disability or made fun of, or bullied by peers which will lower their self-esteem.

- **Communication**

In collaborative work, communication plays a very prominent role. Each one of the group must be given a fair chance to express their ideas. Methods of communication must be clear and consistent. To work well with a group, one has to communicate efficiently.

Collaborative work among Educators & Parents has numerous benefits. A few of them are discussed below:

- Parent involvement means the communication of the parent with the educator in a meaningful way involving the learner's academic learning and overall behavior in the school.
- When educators and parents work in a team, it can reinforce positive behavior and efficient learning skills developed in the classroom. They learn to value education and get support both inside and outside the classroom.

- Improves classroom behavior and enhances the academic performance of the learner.
- Encouragement of parents results in learner's attitude towards school, classroom, and educators.
- Parental involvement lifts educator morale.
- Parental involvement benefits both learners and parents. Parents gain a better understanding of the school curriculum, activities and communicate better with their kids.
- Learners from different cultural backgrounds can get better with their performance when parents and educators collaborate to bridge the gap between home and school learning.
- Time constraint is a greater barrier to parental involvement.

Learning Domains — Bloom's Taxonomy

Bloom's taxonomy was introduced by Benjamin Bloom in 1956. It discusses the **levels of thinking**. It was developed in favor of educators and learners. It helps the educators understand and identify the **level of thinking** in their learners. It also aids the educators in what measures have to be taken for enhancing the learners thinking ability (from lower-order thinking skills to higher-order thinking skills).

Bloom's taxonomy is a classification of three hierarchical models. These models are used to classify educational learning into levels of convolution and meticulosity. The complexity and specificity of the three learning domains discussed by bloom are; **cognitive, affective & conative.**

1. Cognitive Domain

The Blooms Taxonomy was revised in 2001 by Anderson and Krathwohi. It also took changes in its form; noun to a verb.

It discusses 6 levels of thinking skills. It is often shown in the form of a triangle where the lower thinking skills are at the bottom of the triangle and the higher skills are at the top.

Old Version 1956	New Version 2001
EVALUATION	CREATE
SYNTHESIS	EVALUATE
ANALYSIS	ANALYZE
APPLICATION	APPLY
COMPREHENSION	UNDERSTAND
KNOWLEDGE	REMEMBER

The cognitive domain involves the activities relative to the brain. It is further classified into six subdomains;

Remember:

Recall or revisit the information from long-term memory or prior knowledge. It can also be understood as defining, identifying, recognizing, telling, explaining, reciting, memorizing, illustrating, describing, quote.

Understand:

Comprehending meaning by interpreting and summarizing data. It is defined also as summarizing, interpreting, classifying, comparing & contrasting, inferring, relating, extracting, citing, and paraphrasing.

Apply:

Implementation of the learned, in real-life situations. It is defined also as solving, changing, relating, completing, using, sketching, articulating, discovering, and transferring.

Analyze:

Break the information into smaller portions, understand them, and establish relations among each other. Similar terms to describe are; connect, channelize, relate, devise, illustrate, correlate, distill, categorize, sort, and conclude.

Evaluate:

Making judgments based on the information by rechecking. Some words relating to evaluating are; criticize, reframe, defend, appraise, value prioritize, plan and grade.

Create:

Grouping the elements to form a whole new. Things like designing, modifying, role play, developing, rewriting, pivoting, collaborating, invent come in this category.

Remember, understanding and applying are the lower levels of thinking while analyzing, evaluate and creating are higher levels of thinking.

The cognitive domain of learning also refers to a 3H method of learning. The three H's include

- Head
- Hand
- Heart

This means the involvement of thoughts, actions, and soul is essential in learning.

2. Affective Domain

This domain deals with the 'emotions' of an individual. It has a deeper view of all the emotions like happiness, sadness, anger, fear, the excitement that a learner/ an individual experiences. It is further related to values, motivations, feelings, and attitudes. This domain is further classified into five subdomains.

Internalization:

This domain involves a hierarchically structured triangle that has simper feelings at the bottom, moving towards complex feelings at the top. The process of shifting our effect towards something goes from a point of general awareness to a point where internalizes and constantly guides or controls our behavior is internalization. Transmission towards more complex feelings enhances our character.

The five subdomains involved in the affective Domain are;

Receiving

This level is the bottom-most level of the affective domain. Without this level no learning is possible. Having a positive attitude and an open mind is all about receiving. Without receiving nothing can be understood or remembered. The best way of receiving is, one should have the patience to **listen**. Listening to lectures/speeches attentively, watching a movie, and watching ripples in a pond are some examples.

Responding

This level involves the active involvement of the learner in the learning process. The response to a situation should not be dramatic and timid, whereas it should be sincere and genuine. Well-timed responses provide a trustworthy feel in the learner. The responses should be to the point and also provide useful information. Some examples include giving a speech or presentation, following the procedure, participating in discussions or debates.

Valuing

The ability to see the worth in something or someone is called value. The immature form or simplest form is **desire** and its mature form or complex form is being **responsible**. Planning for the success of the team, working in groups are some of the examples.

Organizing

Prioritizing one's ideas or things and relating them to create a value system is known as organizing. Balancing study-time and play-time efficiently, work-life balance, time management to meet the goals are some examples.

Characterization

The complex state of the affective domain is characterization. It deals with the internalizing values and priorities which determine one's character. Spending quality time with friends and family, being human comes under this category.

3. Conative Domain

This is the domain involving sensory activities. It is also known as **the psychomotor domain**. It deals with the physical senses. The process of activities directing behavior and action is conation. It is further classified into six levels namely;

Reflex movements

These movements are known as involuntary movements. They are automatic responses to the stimulus which does not need the involvement of conscious thoughts. Reflex arcs act as the impulses that occur before it reaches the brain.

Basic movements

These are the general movements that involve daily activities such as sitting, standing, walking, and doing regular activities. These movements involve the consciousness of the brain.

Perceptual abilities

The ability to do work by understanding is called perceptual abilities. Perception involves the extraction of information from presenting stimuli.

Physical abilities

The ability to perform physical tasks involves dynamic strength, gross body coordination, and equilibrium.

Skilled movements

The movements involving work with maximum efficiency and minimum effort are called skilled movements. There should be a fixed target and progressive work to achieve it in a limited time with minimum effort.

Non-Discursive communication

This is defined as the highest level of the conative domain. This is the communication involving **body movements** like gestures, facial expressions, dance movements, and choreographers to express one's thoughts or feelings.

Understanding these three domains by an educator is essential. It helps the educators to enhance the learners thinking ability from lower-order skills to higher-order skills.

Learning Styles — Gardner's Theory of Multiple Intelligences

The capability of doing things in one's unique style of thought process is referred to as intelligence. Most of the intelligence is acquired by birth. It cannot be altered, wherein few may be adapted by observation of the environment. We are all born with intellectual potential.

Different people have perceptions towards the same thing in a different way. This resembles that each one of us are having varied thoughts about the same thing. Similarly, every learner has a unique style of learning. This observation of **Howard Gardner** led to the suggestion of the 'theory of intelligence'. Firstly he wrote about this theory in his book **'Frames of Mind'** in 1983.

His suggestions mainly focused on –

- Teaching can be done in more than one way.
- People have diversified learning styles.

He categorized the multiple intelligences into 8 types:

1. Linguistic Intelligence:

Using language to present oneself, expression of ideas & feelings, or persuade others this skill is required. The person remarkable in this skill has good vocabulary in his writings. Teachers, orators, readers, writers, and participants of debate & discussion come in this category.

Swami Vivekananda and Chetan Bhagath are a few prominent personalities with linguistic intelligence.

2. Logical Intelligence

Perceiving skills in mathematical and scientific thinking is logical intelligence. A person possessing skills in problem-solving, reasoning comes in this category.

A.P.J.Abdul Kalam and Sakuntala Devi are a few prominent personalities with logical intelligence.

3. Spatial Intelligence

Skills in forming three-dimensional visual images and patterns are spastically intelligent people. These include sculptors, architects, painters, fashion designers

MF. Hussain and Mokshagundam Visvesvaraya are a few prominent personalities with Spatial intelligence.

4. Musical Intelligence

Having sensitivity towards musical rhythms and patterns, creating new tunes using a musical instrument or by vocal is called musical intelligence. Music composers, orchestras, singers fall into this category.

Lata Mangeshkar and A.R.Rehaman are prominent musicians in India.

5. Bodily-Kinesthetic Intelligence

Expressing feelings physically, by using whole or part of the body flexibility is bodily-kinesthetic. Doing hands-on activities, playing, chopping vegetables include fine & gross motor skills. Sportspersons, dancers, gymnasts, surgeons are grouped in this category.

P.V.Sindhu and M.S.Dhoni are famous sportspeople of India

6. Intrapersonal Intelligence

Understanding of self is called interpersonal intelligence. It is the ability to have clarity in one's perspectives such as thoughts, feelings, ideas, and decisions. These are philosophical people whose vision is different from many others.

Jiddu Krishnamurthy, Socrates, and Plato are some psychologists.

7. Interpersonal Intelligence

Understanding the needs, priorities, and feelings of others and caring for them is interpersonal behavior. People of this mindset believe in *'service to humanity is service to god'*. Social workers, teachers, nurses, and counselors are sensitive to aspects of others' behavior

Mother Theressa, Mahatreya, and Sadhguru are a few people who cater to the needs of others.

8. Naturalistic Intelligence

Classifying things in nature, understanding nature, and enjoying being in nature to admire the pattern it works. Gardeners, farmers, environmentalists, wildlife photographers, geographic explorers, are sensitive to the features of the natural world.

Salim Ali – 'Birdman of India' is one of the famous personalities in the field of ornithology.

These eight bits of intelligence given by Howard Gardner are different but, they all work together, in numerous combinations making each individual's learning style unique. Though we possess this intelligence in each of us, some are submissive and evolve at a given time, while some intelligence is dominant as they are gifted by birth. But Gardner says all of them can be strengthened.

MI in Classroom

Even in the present day, if asked what *is your child good at?* , parents respond concerning their child's capability in math and science. Our culture and many traditional schooling systems, have an ideology to value linguistic and logical intelligence over others. Prominence is given in developing these areas as well.

As a result of this, learners whose intelligences are dominant in linguistic and logic are considered worthful while learners whose intelligences are dominant in others are not considered worthy. This may create a negative impact on the learner.

The theory of Multiple Intelligence enables us to understand the need to identify the learning style of our learners. With this identification, we can encourage them by incorporating field trips, role-play, group work, debate, and puzzles to enrich their knowledge of the topic.

Providing an opportunity for the learner to discover and develop in various aspects of intelligence can benefit them; from bringing out hidden interests, identifying new talents, developing a positive attitude towards them, becoming confident, being successful and accomplished adults in the field of their interest and choice.

Activities incorporated in MI Classroom

Verbal linguistic MI includes activities involving reading books & poems, preparing speeches, visiting an author, writing script, stories, poetry, and story-telling.

Mathematical logical MI includes exercises such as; problem-solving, counting, calculating, computer programming, and solving brainstorming puzzles.

Musical MI includes listening to music, composing &performing in music and dance, playing an instrument, singing, and attending a concert.

Visual-Spatial MI includes artworks like; painting, drawing, photography, graphic designing, slide display, poster making, and visiting an art gallery

Bodily-Kinesthetic MI includes exercises, rhythmic exercises, performance in sports competitions.

Interpersonal MI focuses on team or group work. It also includes plays, panels, and debates.

Intrapersonal MI focuses on reflection time. Investing time on self, such as meditation, remembering memories, changing behavior and habits are some activities included.

Naturalist MI includes activities mostly outside the classroom. It includes a nature walk, caring for plants and animals, farm visits, and botanical garden visits.

Traditional activities focus on linguistic and logical intelligence. These should be expanded to include other intelligence in the classroom as well. Educators with diversified knowledge and creativity will bring all the MI into the classroom for the benefit of learners.

The outcome of including MI in the classroom

Educators must take the initiatives to implement MI in their classrooms. Proper implementation of MI will have positive results in learners.

- Learners develop and demonstrate:
- Sense of accountability
- Self-motivated

- Independent thinking
- Reduced disciplinary issues
- Development of new skills
- A cooperative work style establishes
- Academic achievement

Multisensory Teaching-Learning

Education is the process of learning. There are numerous ways in which learning happens. Learning may be done by instruction or activity or by sharing experiences that involve cognitive, affective, and conative domains. The essence of learning and the process of acquiring knowledge is possible through the senses.

It is proved that knowledge acquired by senses is vital than any other medium. Our senses are considered to be the gateway for acquiring knowledge. Learning with the help of the senses is a natural way of acquiring knowledge. It is highly recommended for pre-primary and primary learners.

When an object is given to kids below 6 years of age, they hold and play with it, making sounds of it. They also taste or byte it, look closely and observe it, and finally learn about it. All these happen through the employment of senses.

Researches have shown results that we learn through our senses as follows:

- 1.5% through TOUCH
- 3.5% through SMELL
- 8% though VISION
- 10% through TASTE
- 11% through HEARING

Multisensory teaching involves more than one sense in the teaching process. This helps the learner to understand the topic in a better way. As we know each learner has a unique way of learning, this approach of teaching will justify the multiple ways of learning possible in the classroom.

Techniques involved in Multisensory teaching

- **Visual:** Use of posters, videos, visual creative design, painting, and drawings
- **Auditory:** Use of music, songs, rhymes, lecture
- **Smell:** use of sensing the smell to perceive or detect something by its scent or order.
- **Tactile:** Involving touch learning, learning by doing, experiments, jigsaw puzzles, Rubik's cube.
- **Kinesthetic:** Use of body parts in teaching-learning. It is specially used while teaching sporting skills.

Characteristics of Multisensory teaching:

- Change in monotonous teaching style.
- Involves more than one sense.
- Helps learners to discover their appropriate learning style.
- Effective for differently-abled learners.
- Helpful for educators dealing with an inclusive classroom
- Easy way of understanding new concepts for learners
- Helps the learner actively participate in the learning process as they involve their whole body in learning
- Learning by doing is encouraged in this process of teaching
- It enables the educator to evaluate their learners who have different strengths in multisensory learning

Educators need to understand the importance of multisensory teaching and employ it in their lesson planning to make the teaching-learning process effective and reliable.

Classroom Discourses

Classroom discourse is referred to as the communication or interaction between learner and educator in the classroom. It involves - teaching process, talking on a topic, discussions, debate, doubts clarification, verbal or written conversation in the classroom. These routines need to be taught to the learner with utmost explicitly to achieve its effect.

Types of Classroom Discourses

- **Narrative**

Narrating a situation, story, or incident dramatically is called narration. Aspects involved in narration are

- ✓ Creativity
- ✓ One's perspective
- ✓ Character imagination
- ✓ Setting a plot
- ✓ Conflict and resolution

- **Description**

Describing the situation as if one feels to be almost present in, and experiencing it. This skill involves sensory images, words & phrases which brings the reality of the situation.

- **Expository**

This method is mainly used to give information about a topic/ story/ situation. It discusses the cause and effect of the happenings.

- **Persuasive**

Persuasive speeches/writings influence the thoughts of a person. It is the smart idea used to convince the person to change their mode of thinking and take action as per the writer or speaker. It always relates to emotions.

- ✓ Advertisements
- ✓ Campaigns
- ✓ Counseling

- **Argumentative**

This is imposing or forcing one's thoughts on others. The views of the argument are put forward in a manner so that the person has no chance to defend it, and so has to accept the speaker. It has few facts involved in the discussion.

Educator's role is to maintain the decorum of the classroom while the activities take place. It is in the hands of the educator to allow the discussions, debates, talking on a topic to happen in a polite way which evolves a healthy learning atmosphere. It is significant to give an ear to learners' talk, give attention to their opinions, give suggestions to their ideas for the betterment, and still be able to maintain the interest in classroom discourses.

Some more techniques of Classroom discourses

- Working in groups – Project work
- Discussions and debates
- Interactive sessions
- Role-play
- Soliloquies interaction
- Topic web

This idea of involving discourses in the classroom evokes learners to develop and improve in varied skills like reading, writing, speaking, comprehending, use of language, critical thinking, evaluating thinking, logical thinking, and also creates scope to know about them.

Classroom Interaction

Objectives of interaction in the classroom

- Classroom interaction aims at meaningful communication among learners and educators.
- This practice helps the educator to assist the learner with clarification of doubts and questions pertaining to a topic.
- It guides the learner to communicate with peers and also in a group.
- It helps the learner to identify their methods of learning

Types of Classroom Interactions

- **Educator-Learner**

This is an interaction that goes one on one. Here the educator communicates with only one learner, be it doubt clarification, re-teach of a concept that is difficult, council the learner regarding behavior, etc. in this interaction, the educator is very active, the learner is mainly receptive. This method suits well for slow learners and for those who feel shy to talk in front of the entire class.

- **Educator-Learners**

This type of interaction may happen in the classroom while the educator addresses the entire class or to a particular group of learners. In this interaction, the learners are passive while the educator is active.

- **Educator & Learner**

This is an interaction in which both the educator and the learners are. This can be a classroom having a discussion platform, introduction/summary of a topic wherein both educators and learners participate to express ideas actively.

- **Learner-Educator**

In this interaction, the learner is active while the educator is a listener. The learner may express personal or classroom issues in person with the educator. The learner may also express ideas of projects or assignments about academics and seek assistance.

- **Learners-Educator**

In this interaction, the learners are active while the educator is a listener. The learners may submit their class ideas to their educator.

Need for classroom interaction

Interaction is a two-way process. The clarity in the teaching-learning process is achieved by the participation of both educators & learners in regular interaction. Learners also gain the confidence to present themselves in front of a group. All learners of the class will be equally benefited in this process.

Classroom Questioning

It is the universally used activation technique in teaching mainly within the initiation-Response-Feedback. It is the educator's tool to revise & summarize a chapter, probe for digging deep into the topic and prompt for eliciting correct answers from the learners.

An educator's questioning should be a balancing mixture of convergent, divergent, and probing questions. The educator should listen to the responses of learners, redirect them with necessary feedback if required or appreciate them for a correct answer. Johnson, Markle & Haley researched in 1987 and presented that – about 40 % of the time is spent in question response mode.

The questioning is mainly one-sided (educator asks questions and learners respond), but in recent times researches tell that questioning is two-sided (educator asks questions learners respond, learners ask questions educators respond)

Reason for Questioning

- To stimulate thinking in learners.
- To make classroom teaching interactive session.
- To find out learners' ideas, views, facts.
- To check or test the knowledge or skill of learners.
- To make learners active.
- Direct the attention of learners to the topic taught.
- To provide a fair chance to all the learners especially the slow learners.

- To encourage thinking and probe more deeply into the topic.
- To allow expression of self-thought.

Criteria of effective questioning

- Clarity
- Learning value
- Interest
- Availability
- Extension
- Educator reaction

Strategies adopted by Educators using Probing Questions

- Educators have to be prepared well in advance on the concept of discussion and questioner.
- They should be estimating on the learner's
- They must be prepared with an explanation along with the critical thinking process.
- Educators have to identify possible misconceptions and misunderstandings of instructions.
- They have to monitor learners, give feedback and evaluate them accordingly.
- Group work may also be enabled while questioning.
- They ask extended thinking questions to enhance thinking skills.

Successful implementation of probing questions in the classroom

- Educators must be passionate regarding the topic to be discussed in the class and engage learners with productive questions.

- The topic to be discussed must be interesting, informative, and thought-provoking.
- Educators must make sure that all the learners involve in the discussion and get a fair chance to answer the probing questions.
- The educator must take charge of the disciplinary issues during questioner sessions.
- The classroom may be bifurcated into pairs or groups to incorporate collaborative work among learners.
- The educator must be ready with the set of questions in relevance with the topic.

Few examples of probing questions:

- Explain in detail......
- Illustrate with examples........
- Do you agree... give a reason why?
- Describe with a real-life application ....

Types of Questioning

According to Patrica Blosser's idea in his book 'How to Ask Right Questions', there are four types of posing questions to the learners in the classroom.

Question Type	Description
Managerial	Enables the educator to maintain the learning of the topic in the same phase.
Rhetorical	Enables to reinforce an idea or emphasis on a point that is a part of the revision of the topic.
Closed	For checking retention or to evaluate the thinking of the learners

Open	Allow the educator to promote debate and discussion. It invites new ideas from the learners

Herbel-Eisenmann & Breyfogie discussed two types of classroom questioning. They named the two techniques as focusing and funneling questions.

Focusing Questioning:

These questions help in thinking deeper into the topic. They focus on reasoning, investigation, description, explanation, predictions, assumptions, and more. This type of question leads to the diversified thinking of the learner. It would make the learner curious about the topic and help them to explore the topic for more information.

A few example questions are:

- From where could you begin the investigation?
- What are your findings from the experiment?
- How do you think it works? Explain.
- Is there another method to do and get the same result?
- How can we relate these?

Funnel Questioning:

Funneling questions reflect on guiding the learners towards the way chosen by the educator. It is guided practice. This is a convergent way of questioning where there is only one procedure to arrive at its solution. In this type, the learner may not have scope for exploring and finding new aspects of the topic.

A few example questions are:

- What will be the result if you try this method?
- So you will find this first.
- What if you did this instead of that?

Practical Approaches Involved in Teaching-Learning

Methods of teaching are diverse all around the world. These approaches are designed by educationalists and psychologists based on certain principles and guidelines. Effective teaching and learning are possible in a child-centered classroom where active participation of learners is enabled. These procedures were suggested and adapted for successful teaching and learning process after research. Hence it is required for an educator, to know the practical approaches, which are proven best, to incorporate in their classrooms as per the requirement (about grade and average understanding level of the class).

Inductive & Deductive approach

- **The inductive method** is a psychological method in which a standard fact is considered to be true and generalized equations are made saying that, the fact implies true for rest.
- It proceeds from concrete facts to abstract rules.
- It gives scope for experimentation and discovery. Hence it helps the learner to attain clarity on the topic.
- **The deductive method** is an application-based approach that leads from abstract principle to concrete example.
- It enhances speed and efficiency in solving problems on repeated practice.

Analytical & Synthetic

- **The analytical method** is logical. Analysis means to split a problem into small meaningful parts to understand it. This method proceeds from **unknown to known**.
- It provides learners to have better understanding and clarity in the concept.
- **Synthesis** means to combine or place together with the parts that are apart.
- This method proceeds from **known to unknown**. This is a psychological method.

Laboratory method

- This method is an extension of the induction method. It proceeds from the concrete to the abstract.
- Learning by doing is referred to as the best method of teaching in which the learner retains the concept for a long duration.
- According to researchers when learners are allowed to experiment with the guidance of educators, they gain more knowledge and their remembrance level is also high.
- This is a learner-centered approach where the educator demonstrates and later guides.
- There is a need to understand the importance of this approach and provide laboratory facilities to languages, mathematics, social studies, and sciences by the management.

Heuristic method

- This method is followed by scientists and inventors. It is the method of discovery originated by Prof. Amstrong.

- This method aims to inculcate self-thinking, independent judgment, originality of work in learners.
- The educator plays a vital role in this method who should be resourceful and aims to cultivate a heuristic spirit in learners.
- The questions asked should be thought-provoking which motivates the learner to think innovatively.
- The educator is required to have patience and alertness while dealing with this approach.

Project method

- The realistic application of classroom knowledge is called the project method. It requires observation, creativity, and proper execution of the plan.
- This is a learner-centered approach, where educator needs to guide and evaluate their work.
- The educator may give group/team projects to develop team spirit among learners.
- It involves five steps
  - ✓ Planning
  - ✓ Execution
  - ✓ Evaluation
  - ✓ Recording
  - ✓ Conclusion

Activity method

- The activity method is based on the concept 'learning by doing.
- In this method, the educator encourages both individual and team/group learning.
- Educators need to plan prior for open-ended, creative, and manipulative activities for the learners.

- Problem-solving, critical thinking, and creativity of learners are exhibited in this method.
- This method develops self-learning

Concept attainment model – Jerome Burner

- This method is indirect. It was proposed by Jerome Burner.
- It includes a structured inquiry process.
- It helps learners to connect between what they know and what they learn from the process.
- It enables the learner to examine the given task from various perspectives and come to a valid conclusion.
- It helps in making learners understand the concept by giving examples of their knowledge, by which concept is learned thoroughly.

There are certain steps an educator needs to follow to incorporate this approach of teaching:

- ✓ Define the concept
- ✓ Select varied attributes
- ✓ Give positive and negative examples
- ✓ Give learners a nutshell of the concept
- ✓ Give some more examples if required
- ✓ Elicit learners understanding of the concept
- ✓ Evaluate

Active Classroom vs Passive Classroom

Case study: Science Lesson

Classroom A

It is a science class. Class A has 25 learners listening to their educator. The educator poses a question to the class to elicit the topic name –

'Name the parts of a tree. Each learner gives their answer like stem, leaves, branches, flowers, fruits, roots, etc. The educator announces that we shall learn 'parts of a flower today.

The educator shows a hibiscus flower (which was brought as TLM) and starts naming the parts by dissecting and showing them to the learners. The class is then divided into groups and each group is given a hibiscus flower. Learners are instructed to dissect the flower and name its parts.

Active participation was observed among the learners. Occasionally, learners called educators for help. Summarizing the class, the educator conducts a quiz on the topic. All learners were eager to answer (without the help of the educator). Learners had great fun learning the topic.

Classroom B

It is a science class. Class B has 25 learners listening to their educator. The educator announces the topic 'Parts of a Flower' and starts to draw the diagram with colorful chalk pieces and labels the parts. Meanwhile, she instructs the learners to open their textbook page number (45).

On completing the drawing, she calls upon learners' names randomly and asks them to read the textual paragraph, and explains each sentence in detail showing the diagram on the board.

Summarizing the class, the educator questions the learners randomly, where ever the learner gives a wrong answer, the educator gives the correct one.

Report of the case study:

Classroom A	Classroom B
• Learner Centered class	• Teacher Centered class
• Active participation of learners	• Passive participation of learners
• Interactive class room	• Non- Interactive classroom
• learning from peers	• No peer learning
• Group work – improving behavior and communication skills	• No group work
• Real life application	• Visualization of diagram
• Do it yourself and learn	• See and learn

Remembrance levels

Educator centered classroom	Learner-Centered classroom
10% of what is read	50% of what is seen & heard
20% of what is heard	70 % of what is spoken aloud
30% of what is seen	90% of what is performed

Therefore a learner-centered classroom is an active classroom in which the learner gets scope for involving, doing, expressing ideas, and discussing with educator & peers as well. This way of acquiring knowledge is most essential for incorporating classroom learning in real-life scenarios.

A passive classroom restricts the learner from acquiring the knowledge practically. This may further obstruct the application of knowledge in the real world.

Mind – Congenial Classroom

It is the responsibility of every educator to make their classroom resourceful, interesting, thoughtful, and also entertaining. A classroom blended with all these elements will produce a wonderful learning platform. Such a classroom is just like a complete meal.

The classrooms which have their teachings, aspiring to make their learners **'think and explore'** are always referred to as mind congenial. These are the platforms where the learner has the liberty to express views, understand by doing hands-on activities and experiments. In such environments, the learner's mental ability strengthens and they will be prepared to face the challenges ahead.

Here are some methods to conduct a mind-congenial classroom

Interactive

The class must always be learner-centered. It should include activities like quizzes, role-play, just a minute (JAM), pep-talk. The educator's focus should be that every learner of the class is participating in the activity and acquiring knowledge on the topic. This model of class can be compared to a hockey match where learners are the players and the educator is the match referee.

Real-life applications

Complete knowledge of a topic can be attained only if it is related to our daily activities. The educator has to be more vigilant while giving examples for a topic. While teaching about projectile, the educator can include the game cricket and explain about throw and catch. Similarly while explaining fractions, the educator can the example of a pizza. These acts enhance the creativity of the learners.

Multiple intelligences

The educator should be aware that all learners do not have the same skill of grasping things. There should be at least 2 multiple intelligences involved in the classroom teaching. Inclusion of Kinesthetic activities includes body & mind connection may be chosen as one of the multiple intelligences. Researches proved that many learners are inclined towards kinesthetic activities.

Challenging

The tasks assigned to the learners like projects/worksheets should be challenging. It should follow the path **known to unknown**. It should include the application of classroom learning and also be interesting. The educator should also take care that the task assigned should be challenging but not difficult, such that every learner will be able to complete the task.

Group work and collaboration

Group work enables the learners to establish a healthy relationship with their peers. In this collaboration, new ideas emerge and the learning would be successful. There is a possibility of domination or bullying if a selection of groups is not proper. The educator must make the groups in such a way that there is a gifted learner, an average learner, and a slow learner together in a group. No group should be given special preference and the learners should not be tagged.

Technology

Audio Visual (AV) aids can be used to enhance learning. AV is generally used for summarizing a topic. Online quizzes, goggle forms, online debates can be conducted to enhance the learning ability.

Ambiance

The classroom is itself a tool for the teaching-learning process. Its walls, pinboards, soft boards, etc. should be informative. The educator should take the opportunity of decorating the classroom with student works and projects. Apart from students' work, news- headlines, charts (about respective grades) should be set up. This makes the classroom the best place for the learners to be.

Activities kids must do for better brain health

Inculcate a healthy lifestyle: Eating habits play a prominent role in the physical and mental wellbeing of a kid. So, healthy food habits must be inculcated from childhood. A well-planned and organized day is a part of a healthy lifestyle.

Learn cognitive skills: These are the skills that keep the kid agile and stimulate development. It helps in keeping the mind always active.

Solve puzzles and Brainteasers: Along with being active, it is important to be smart. Solving puzzles and brain teasers develops the brain to function with higher dopamine levels.

Focus on Math: This develops cognitive skills, analyzing, problem-solving and deduction skills. It helps the brain to function actively and keeps the person attentive all the time.

Introduce to physical activity: Kids should be involved in yoga or any other physical activity. It should be made mandatory for kids between 3years to 14 years because their physical growth happens in this age group. Strength and agility in bones furnish in this age. Apart from this, mental health also happens crucially at this age. The behavioral characteristics, personality enhancement will be framed perfectly when the kind is involved in regular physical activity. It benefits for a lifetime.

Learn a new language: In early childhood, kids have more grasping than adults. They learn by observation and imitation. A new language along with mother tongue has to be taught in the early years. it is beneficial as that can be learned and adapted by the kid easily. It eventually activates the brain in learning new things.

We might have experienced in our life, the things we learned in our schooling are easy to perform and handle. And we remember it for a lifetime. But, after schooling or being an adult, if we are interested to learn something new, we need more concentration and time.

Engage in creative skills: Arts are the rich form of creativity. Painting, drawing, sculpture, clay art, theater, dance, music are some examples of creative skills. In some kids creative skills are inherited yet detailed in the skill is acquired only through regular practice. These creative skills make the brain feel happy, relaxed, calm, and young. Participation in creative skills is a sign of happiness to every individual.

Flip Classroom

Flip Classroom is generally defined as a classroom where "Home task is done at school and school task is done at home". It shifts the classroom from passive to active. Higher-order thinking skills are mainly focused in this approach by evaluating, analyzing, creating, and meaningful engagement of learners.

It is an approach in which interactive learning is aimed. This approach relies on understanding the difference between acquiring information and knowledge providing learners with active learning possibilities. The educator's role is to guide during the application of concepts and creatively engage the learners.

Many educators might have incorporated flip classes in their teaching by encouraging learners to read text outside the class, watch instructional content videos. There are four pillars of the Flipped classroom:

Flexible environment

- The educator needs to establish spaces and time frames that allow learners to interact and reflect on their learning as needed.
- The educator must always observe and monitor students to make adjustments to their work as appropriate.
- The educator should provide learners with different ways to learn content and demonstrate mastery.

Learning culture

- Educators must give their learners opportunities to engage in meaningful activities with the child being central.
- I scaffold these activities and make them accessible to all students through differentiation and feedback.

Intentional content

I prioritize concepts used in direct instruction for learners to access on their own. I create and/or curate relevant content (typically videos) for my students. I differentiate to make content accessible and relevant to all students.

Professional educators

I make myself available to all students for individual, small group, and class feedback in real-time as needed. I conduct ongoing formative assessments during class time through observation and by recording data to inform future instruction. I collaborate and reflect with other educators and take responsibility for transforming my practice

Strategies to implement in Flipped Classroom

Assign learners with questions to answer

- Ask learners to answer a few questions about the readings to then review in class
- Questions can be the same or different
- Divide Groups
- Clear the misconceptions and normalize the situation
- More time in discussions and activities about the topic
- Instead of reading in class we can startup in-depth discussions

Create lecture videos

- Record videos and upload them to the class website for the learners to watch at any time.
- Learners will receive all required information needed and thus class time can be utilized in doing activities or discussions.
- Classes can be recorded while teaching a set of learners to save time.
- Remember that the syllabus may change timely but concept and content will remain the same
- Recordings can be used further to make flipped learning more effective.
- These recordings will be of great benefit to absentees and also learners who require repetition of class.

Provide Demonstration videos

- For topics discussed and explained in the classroom, demonstration videos can be sent with clear instructions that, they would be discussed and questioned in the next class.
- These demonstration videos may include a science and mathematics experiment, case study, survey report, and graphical representations
- Educator has to suggest the demonstration video to be watched to avoid unnecessary confusion in the concept
- In a complete flipped classroom, along with lecture videos, demonstration videos need to be sent.

Create an online class - group discussion

- Hosting digital discussions is another way to flip the classroom

- Often educators notice that the learners who are not comfortable answering in offline class are expressive in an online class
- The educator sets up starter questions to spark/ initiate the discussion and encourage learners to discuss their questions under the educator's guidance.
- You can include guest speakers

Flipped Classroom games

To make the concept even clearer, the following are a few strategies that can be practiced in the classroom

- **Group quizzes** group consist a maximum of four learners.

When questions are asked, the group has to discuss and give an answer. Individual answers are not encouraged.

- **Oxford-Style debate**

This activity can be practiced based on the requirement of the topic or subject.

Every learner of the class makes a T-chart and notes the **for & against** points of the debate. This debate will be concluded by educator

- **Group Crossword puzzle**

The educator must be ready with different crossword puzzles on the topic.

Dividing the class into groups, the educator must issue the crossword puzzle sheet to each group.

Time-bound completion has to be instructed.

- **Role Play**

In subjects like social and English, role play is effective.

Learners need to be given characters and clear instructions on their performance.

Thinking Skills

"Thinking is an implicit problem-solving behavior" – Mohsin (1967). It is a Cognitive process that involves elements like — thinking, memory, retention, organizing information, planning, evaluating ideas, creating display/working models. It has an influence on thought processes & actions and learning abilities as well. Here are some important thinking skills.

- **Convergent Thinking**

The thinking which focuses on only one outcome is convergent. It is the tool used in creative problem-solving. Solving multiple-choice questions is an example of convergent thinking, where only one option among the four is correct and we need to eliminate the wrong ones. It is a skill that does not need significant creativity to answer a standard question.

- **Divergent**

The process of thinking which involves creativity, exploration, results drawn from experiments, etc is divergent thinking. Many possible ideas are drawn to a problem in a limited time by exploring is called thinking divergent. This type of thinking is seen in individuals with personality traits such as nonconformity, curiosity, risk-taking, and persistence.

To enhance one's divergent thinking, it is to evoke creativity in them. The ability to recollect and connect concepts stored in long-term memory to the present situation and get a valid solution quickly is the most efficient way of thinking.

Factors of Divergent thinking

- **Difficulty level** — Understanding the complexity of the problem and thinking of innovative ways to solve it.
- **Interest** — Showcasing curiosity to know more about the problem, drawing information, learning by questioning and thinking of various possibilities.
- **Development** — Skill of giving inputs & adding content to the existing idea and thus enhancing its value.
- **Flexibility** — Skill of incorporating new ideas to have numerous solutions for a given problem
- **Imagine** — Ability to visualize dreams
- **Authenticity** — Skill of coming up with one's ideas or unique stuff.
- **Daring** — Being bold enough, challenging, and courageous to perform experiments, surveys to differentiate between self and others.

Divergent thinking is the overall art of new ideas, innovations, and creativeness and can be developed in learners at early stages by identifying their interests

- **Critical Thinking**

The ability to have clarity in thought, by a perfect understanding of a situation or a problem is critical thinking. It improves the quality of ideas and comprehension abilities. It helps in evaluating ideas and choosing the best among them.

Some key elements of individuals possessing critical thinking are

- ✓ Connecting ideas logically.
- ✓ Identify, construct and evaluate arguments.
- ✓ Detect inconsistency in reasoning.
- ✓ Systematic problem-solving.

- ✓ Identification of significance and relativeness in ideas.
- ✓ Analyze & justify one's beliefs and ideas.

- **Problem-solving**

The thinking ability which involves overcoming hurdles, collecting information, making assumptions, and taking decisions is called problem-solving. reasoning, decision making, creative thinking, critical thinking are all the factors of problem-solving. They all are interlinked with one another.

Steps involved in Problem Solving are:
- ✓ Understand the problem
- ✓ Collecting and sorting information /data collected
- ✓ Evaluating/ making assumptions
- ✓ Arriving at a valid conclusion

- **Decision making**

Decision-making is otherwise called choice making. This is an activity for all of us in our daily routine. It is the process of making choices by setting goals. The choice may be personal or influenced by a situation/ circumstances.

Steps involved in Decision making are:
- ✓ Purpose of the choice
- ✓ Collecting information pertaining to the choice
- ✓ Finding the possible alternatives
- ✓ Evaluation of all alternatives
- ✓ Selection of the best alternative
- ✓ Execution
- ✓ Evaluate the outcome

Thinking skills differ in every individual. These skills are applied to make sense of an experience. These skills also permit us to compare and contrast between, situations taking place around us. Better thinking will allow us to not only become successful in learning but will also equip us for life. It entitles us to realize our interests and potential.

Importance of 'Planning for Instruction'

Planning is needed to perform a task or event hassle-free. In our daily routine, we plan events like parties, functions, get-togethers, and marriage.

We also plan regarding education, career, up-gradation in economy and more. For all deeds to happen positively in life planning and execution are very important.

In teaching, planning and proper execution leads to the successful realization of objectives and channelize time and energy in the right way.

Proper planning of lessons, activities, projects, assignments, worksheets, handouts, and assessments by educators will enhance the teaching-learning process and benefit the learner.

Academic planning is broadly classified into three categories

Year Plan/Annual Plan

It is the plan of the entire syllabus that has to be covered in the academic session. All subject educators should do it before the academic session initiates.

- The educator must be aware of the number of working days and holiday lists for designing the annual plan. Each unit /chapter may be given a tentative month for completion of teaching.
- With this planning, the educator can have a nutshell of the entire syllabus and when & how it would be taught.

- The educator must make sure that the year plan includes analysis of the unit/chapter, instructional objectives, number of periods required for teaching.
- It helps the educator in optimum utilization of time and available resources to proceed with systematic teaching.

Unit Plan

The unit plan is defined as dividing the entire syllabus into small meaningful blocks /portions and planning for what actually will be taught in each block.

- Educators need to be smart to divide each unit into smaller portions called sub-units.
- The educator must plan for what activities, experiments, demonstrations will be essential for teaching the unit.
- The educator must have clarity of TLM's, and other materials needed that would make learners curious about the unit.
- Educators need to keep the material ready at least a day before classroom teaching.
- Methods of evaluation also need to be selected as per the needs of the unit

Lesson Plan

Many of us feel that after the year plan and unit plan, "what is the use of writing lesson plan?". But the key to day-to-day teaching lies in the lesson plan. It is the comprehensive unit plan where the educator plans for each of her classes.

If an educator arrives at the class without prior preparation, the utilization of time will not be done aptly thus ruining the purpose of the class. The educator may have many years of experience in teaching, but planning a lesson for the day will enrich the quality of classroom teaching.

The lesson plan is a plan of action designed by the educator. It not only includes the method adapted in teaching the topic, if keenly observed, it includes educator's creativity, ability to adapt effective methods, and understanding the learners.

A lesson plan is an outline of the important points of the lesson arranged in an order in which they are to be presented by the educator – **Good. C.V**

Few Pros of Lesson Planning:

- Objectives of the lesson/topic are achieved with less effort.
- Can make the class interesting, interactive, and encouraging for learners.
- Achieve time management.
- Boosts up self-confidence and self-satisfaction in educators.
- Thought-provoking Home tasks and worksheets can be prepared.

Sequence in LesonPlan

Johan Fiat Rich Herbert (1776-1841) was a German Philosopher. He performed various researches on pedagogy and philosophy and framed guidelines for planning lessons. His suggestions were named 'Herbartian steps for lesson planning.

Herbartian approach includes six steps:

1. Preparation
In this step, the educator tests the prior knowledge of learners by asking questions to start up with the present lesson /topic. Educator tries to elicit a few known facts from the learners as a part of the introduction.

2. Presentation
This stage involves the actual teaching-learning process; delivery of content. Educator demonstrates and explains the concepts of the lesson using different TLM's and teaching strategies as planned.

3. Comparison
In this stage, the educator relates prior knowledge of learners with the present concept being taught in the class. It is incorporating the known facts into the newly learned.

4. Generalization
Educator gives many examples to make the concept more clear. I this stage the clarity of concept is achieved. Learners are also given opportunities to express their ideas to generalize the concept.

5. Application
After dealing with theoretical examples, the generalized concept is further proceeded to apply in real-life situations. On practical application, knowledge becomes more meaningful to the learner.

6. Recapitulation/ Evaluation
This step was included in later stages and is not the primitive Herbartian approach. The concept is revisited by summarizing it by the educator. Further learners are tested by questioning, pen-paper test, conducting quizzes, and presentations. This will enhance the self-learning ability of the learner and also through the concept.

In the present scenario, few amendments are made to the Herbartian approach of lesson planning proposed by SCERT.

They are referred to as Phases of Teaching:

- ✓ **Introductory Activity:** It includes **the Preparatory** step of the Herbartian approach
- ✓ **Development Activity:** It includes **the Comparison** step
- ✓ **Cumulative Activity: Generalization Application & Evaluation** is grouped into this activity

Classroom Management

Classroom management is referred to as the strategies an educator uses to maintain the discipline and dignity of the classroom. These strategies may involve elements that help the educator in keeping the learners focused on a given task, being organized, attentive all the time, using polite words, maintaining etiquette, and being academically productive.

It is generally understood that an effective and experienced educator is skilled & equipped well to manage a class, then a new inexperienced or ineffective educator. Classroom management may affect the teaching-learning process. And hence every educator should mandatorily know about how best a class can be managed productively.

Classroom management is one of the most fearful parts of teaching for educators new to the teaching field. If a class cannot be engaged productively, it causes stress for an educator resulting in deciding to leave this noble profession.

The latest idea of classroom management extends to everything that an educator does in facilitating & mentoring the learners to enhance their learning, which includes elements like –

- **Conduct**: Positive affirmations, encouraging statements, respectful & fair treatment of learners, etc.
- **Habitat**: Intellectually stimulating
- **Anticipation**: Behavior among peers, respect to educators & elders.
- **Resources**: Providing equipment, learning resources

An educator's unprepared class, poorly designed lesson plans, uninteresting activities cause disinterest in the learners thus creating a disorganized classroom. Every move of the educator affects the classroom and the behavior of learners. An effective teaching and effective classroom management are inseparable.

The best way to be a successful classroom manager is, to understand the needs and priorities of the learners. Educators must always maintain a healthy relationship with their learners. Social-emotional learning has an impact on the quality of the educator-learner relationship. In a well-managed classroom, the learning is fruitful and academic goals are achieved.

In real-time practice, classroom-management techniques seem to be effortless, but, integrating them successfully into the instruction of learners typically requires a lot of sophisticated techniques and a significant amount of patience, skill, and experience.

In the book 'Elements of Classroom Management' written by Joyce McLeod, Jan Fisher, and Ginny Hoover Key, they say — **'A Good classroom management begins with proper planning of the time given /available'**.

The educator must be ready with instructions, lesson planning, activities that are pre-planned for the class which helps in academic learning. It should not be focused on behavior specifically. Such planning involves:

- ✓ Topic relevant handouts.
- ✓ Logic related and problem-solving techniques worksheets/assessments.
- ✓ Brainstorming activities & assignments.
- ✓ Guided Practice.
- ✓ Correction & Feedback.

An educator, who is equipped with teaching skills and a subject expert, can organize lessons in a planned way. They can understand the priority of their learners and hence make arrangements for the class to take place in the right way. An effective instruction helps in reducing problems of classroom behavior but does not uproot it. The learner–educator relationship will enhance the behavior of the learner by reducing some behavior issues.

Some Classroom management practices:

- Engaging learners with interesting and productive work.
- Maintain a distraction-free physical environment.
- No favoritism is to be shown by educators.

Technology

Earlier, phones and tabs were not allowed in school and college, but in today's scenario, the school itself is on digital devices. There are numerous platforms where educators share their knowledge with the learners digitally. Flipped classroom teaching, hybrid classroom, the online classroom has become more prominent methods of teaching these days. Online courses have become popular, and famous universities are offering a few courses in online mode to acquire a degree as well.

Educators need to upgrade themselves to meet the expectations of today's generations. They need to be prepared and well equipped with the technological aspects along with their subject knowledge. The need to implement blended learning by incorporating traditional teaching and technology teaching has emerged.

At the same time, educators need to be crucial in judging whether the 'learner needs better technology or better thinking?' Educators need to be vigilant to check how these technological tools can function to increase the depth of knowledge, clarity in concept, learning curiosity, creativity, and critical thinking skills.

Use of technology in the classroom and challenges encountered

1. Social Media & Websites

Educators share information with the learners about topics, in the form of handouts, reference websites, YouTube videos, and other digital information. They may share the digital content either in the classroom for the whole group, or away from the school project work. This will encourage the learner to develop individuality, work with peers or manage group work, and evolve creativity.

The challenge faced is time management: There should be the usage of social media and websites under the surveillance of adults or parents. As the information is the websites are endless and vast, there will be no time limit for learners to work on the digital content.

2. Reading Programme

Learners having trouble in reading, pronunciation, punctuation, and more opt for online reading programs. These programs are beneficial for beginners. They help in scoring marks in reading skills.

The challenge faced in opting for reading programs is spending lots of money. As the online programs are pre-designed, they don't have a higher order of difficulty reading. Instead, educators need to encourage learners to read books with varied content to improve reading levels. And also incorporate vocabulary acquired in their speaking as well.

3. CBT

A computer-based test is a standard testing pattern accepted officially. This is the latest innovation in the educational field. It helps in the conduction of tests without any hurdles and also the results are declared quickly. Manpower is replaced with digital technology

The challenge faced is that some learners with minimum or nil digital knowledge face a lot of difficulties in clearing/passing a CBT rather than PPT (Pen-Paper Test). The institution has to provide minimum technological facilities to train the learners from rural backgrounds especially. Educators need to conduct CBT mocks frequently to help the learners handle the CBT with confidence.

4. Calculators, Smart-boards

In the classroom, educators use calculators and smart-boards to not only simply engage learners, but also to provide diverse platforms for learners to work with fresh thoughts and demonstrate valued understanding. These tools simplify the educator's work in teaching. Most digital tools permit the educator to deal with real-time, which not only saves time but more critically allows the learner to give immediate feedback.

The challenge faced is learners become lethargic in solving simple calculations and are looking for calculators in smartphones and tablets.

5. LMS

The definition of a **learning management system** has changed over the years, as the working style and elegance of these systems have changed. Today the online classroom platform offered by zoom meetings, Webex, Google classroom, teach mint, and more have become technically LMS. The advantage of incorporating technology in the classroom, curriculum, assessment, and instruction should all be designed to work perfectly with a constantly evolving learning management system.

Challenges faced are expenses incurred in integrating technology in the classroom. Educators need to be trained and upgrade themselves to be tech-savvy.

There may be many more ways in integrating and incorporating technology with the teaching and learning process. But, it should be agreed that by using technology, the educator's ideas and visualization can be well portrayed and projected to the learner to enhance their understanding, but can never replace the educator. So educators need to know their prominence for the future generations and mound themselves to be tech-savvy and upgrade their teaching skills and make their classes realistic.

Giving Feedback

Feedback is the most important part of the teaching-learning process. Educator's responsibility is to check and know how the teaching process has marked an impression in the learner's aspect regarding a chapter/topic.

To carry out this process, educators conduct assessments in varied styles. Assessments can be carried out in a formal way like pen-paper tests, formative assessments, progressive tests, and class tests that can be documented. Assessments can also be carried out informally like random questioner, quiz, group discussion, role-play, and more.

In any of the assessments be it formal or informal, the educator's idea is to understand the learner's **acquired knowledge** in the topic/chapter. With the performance and participation of the learner, the educator needs to give feedback to improve the quality of learning and enhance their skills, and to guide them forward.

Educators need to be fair while giving feedback. They must consider that feedback need not be always positive. Feedback is not only the reflection of learners' academics; it is also regarding, participation in co-curricular activities and their behavior in the school with peers, educators, and helping staff as well. It may include appreciation, instruction, and ideas for a better way of learning, constructive criticism, evaluation, reflection.

Strategies for providing feedback

1. 3C's Feedback

The feedback given should be mind bobbling and refreshing to the learner instead of depressed and demotivating. The three C's feedback includes **Complement Correct Compliment**. This would be like a sandwich that includes the point to be corrected and also imbibes a compliment. This kind of feedback motivates the learner to a '*Go for it !*' attitude.

2. Time-bounded Feedback

The intensity of *waiting for the result* for assessment/competition/sports/games lies in the learner for about 24 to 48 hours. The feedback should be given by an educator/coach along with the result for having a better impact, and to carry it forward in implementation. Time-bounded feedback is always appreciable.

3. Ask the 4 questions ????

Educators new to the teaching platform or educators who are new to a particular class/group of learners struggle in writing feedback. Here are a few suggestive questions which when answered will portray valuable feedback for the learner.

- What is the learner good at?
- What is the learner not good at? Suggestions for improvement.
- How does the learner perform/participate when compared with others?
- How can he improve and do better?

4. Focus on one ability

Educators need to focus on one skill at a time. It helps the learner in mastering the concept rather than confusion. It makes a far greater impact on the learner when only one skill is corrected/ criticized and to achieve mastery on it. Assigning a target and mentoring the learner to attain mastery will be the accomplishment of the task for the day. The Next day/ in the next task, the educator may focus on another skill. In this way, the learner will be able to correct one by one skill with focus and dedication.

5. Note making

In physical classrooms, learners must be advised to make notes of the topic, while the educator discusses in the class regarding corrections and suggestions. This enables the learner to avoid the same error in their next assessments. Note making also helps the learner to remember for a longer time, because the discussion is made after an assessment, which the learner has attempted after preparation.

In digital classrooms, voice recordings of educators can be sent on each assessment either in the class group or personally. Here the learners must be advised to make notes of the corrections and suggestions. This has the same benefits as in the physical classroom.

6. Handle negative feedback

Learners in today's generation are very sensitive. They are not in a position to handle extreme situations either positive or negative. So, educators need to present negative feedback in a very polished way. Educators can express their feedback and give suggestions to overcome them by using post-it notes in the learner's notebooks, talking personally, sending a WhatsApp message, voice recording, and email. This will also help in boosting the learner's confidence and trust in the educator.

The educator must not avoid giving negative feedback whenever required, as we are responsible for their overall development.

7. Positive feedback

Positive feedback or appraisal should be mentioned in front of everyone. This will build an encouraging spirit in the learner. And it will also help other learners of the class to work along the same lines and succeed. The educator needs to be vigilant that the appraisal should not lead to overconfidence in the learner.

8. Higher-order vs. Lower-order

The educator needs to be aware of the higher-order and lower-order concepts of feedback. The higher-order feedback focuses on **content, ideas argument, and thesis**, while the lower order focuses on **grammar, spelling, language, and punctuation**.

This order is applicable while dealing with subjects like mathematics, accounts, physics, and chemistry. While dealing with languages like English, Hindi, literature of local languages, the priority order will alter.

9. Early and short

Educators should be quick in their work and need to give small feedback in a short duration. This is most important for educators. This feedback will enable the learners to make it possible for them to carry forward the feedback in their learning process.

There may be many other ways of giving valuable feedback to the learners. But, the above mentioned will surely help you if implemented the way they are suggested. All these methods are proved to be successful as they are practiced by educationalists.

Educators as Role Model

Learners think of their educators as role models. One of the biggest reasons is the desire to become a role model for learners is to look up to, to learn from, and to remember for the rest of their lives.

Each one of us has felt the power and lasting presence of an effective teacher, who also had a greater impact on our lives. Whether it's learning the value of community service, discovering a love for a particular subject, or how to tap the confidence to speak in public, educators enlighten the way for us in this world.

Educators being role models for their learners is not a new concept. It has inspired learners to go into this field for ages. You can think of becoming a role model. Here are a few tips to be followed to inspire young hearts.

Humble: Children learn by imitation. As an educator being humble is very important, because children try to imitate the way their educator behaves. It is our responsibility to show learners what it is like to be wrong and admit it. And educator has to show them that right is right, and wrong is wrong – no matter what, but in a humble way.

Encourage and respect individualized thoughts: Conducting creative activities in the classroom fosters conversations and makes learners discover them and appreciate each other. The educator must celebrate the learners' diversified thoughts. Trust bond will be developed among the learners and this helps each other in focusing on learning.

Involving in Volunteer activity: Incorporating **voluntary service** in the classroom teaching and encouraging learners to do service in the real world is a way to inculcate the quality of service in their minds. Visit an orphan home, and an old age home are some activities.

Empathy: When learners think of educators as role models, they expect sympathetic mentors who listen to them. All we need to do is 'show that you care for them'. The educator needs to show empathy towards the learners.

Suggestive Behavior: Educators need to create a culture in the classroom that rewards kind behavior. The importance of the educator is positive reinforcement and boosting confidence & behavior. The educator should teach them to be constructive with their criticism, pointing out positives before negatives, or suggestions for improvement.

Keep up your promise: Educators and learners are busy with their works throughout the year. But educators need to remember their promises and keep up the word to be role models. When a promise is made to the class, the educator must be honest and not make excuses. Learners also will see how to deal with their own shortcomings and will respect educators for their honesty.

Social media: Educators shouldn't mix up social media with learners. They should take care of sharing their personal social media accounts with their learners. Educators should have the policy to connect with students only on the channels that the school sets up. They should also remember that 'parents are watching you as well. And know that educators are in a role model position with their children. Just be vigilant.

Physical activity: The significance of the educator extends to the physical fitness of their learners. Physical activity enables learners to be active in the classroom. It doesn't matter if every learner is inclined to be physically active. Encouraging physical activity is good for all groups of learners. Even if one doesn't teach a physical education class, they can still talk about physical activities when performing other classroom activities.

Iconic Profiles: Educators should find a way to incorporate a **hero story** in their class. This will enable learners to discuss ways they can be heroes in their own lives. Educators can also encourage learners to read or watch iconic profiles and learn the characteristics of great personalities. Being a good role model is to show learners how to point their moral compass in the right direction.

Discuss world events: Educators should plan a class in a week to discuss special events around the world. The idea behind sparking discussion is to ask questions and make learners' think. Educators being role models include showing learners how to make sense of the world, and express different ideas in a peaceful way. Educators should see that all learners participate actively in the discussion.

Planning pot luck: Once in a while, having a meal with learners and spending time together is a good sign of a healthy relationship. Food is another way learners see educators as role models. After all, we all love food! So, ask learners that they are welcome to bring a dish from home. This can be a good way to talk about cooking. Be that educator that shows them that learning to cook and eating healthy foods is good for health.

Incorporate ideas of democracy in class discussions: Educators being role models should demonstrate to learners 'how our democracy works'. Hold votes on decisions that reflect discussions on topics to see where learners stand. Then encourage debate and explain to learners 'how our system is supposed to work'. This will enlighten the core values of the learners.

Class garden: Many schools have room for classes to start their own small garden. This can teach learners about growing food, and how people have to work together to sustain our standards of living.

Presentation on one of their role models: Lastly, ask learners to think about what makes a good role model, and present their findings to the class. It can be a famous personality or anyone who inspires them. Try not to frame too many rules.

There must be a million ways that educators can be stand-up as role models for their learners. The above mentioned are a few ideas that may help an educator to become the best role model to their learners.

Educator as Leader

The way to a **child-centered** education can be achieved by **an educator-centered** institution. "No education system can rise higher than its educators". The quality of a nation depends upon the quality of schools and this internally depends upon the quality of educators. This is true because we believe in *"Today's children are the builders of tomorrow's nation"*.

A well-renowned educational report says that – they were convinced that the most important factor in the contemplated educational reconstruction is the educator and their qualities. An educator must possess a well-rounded, cherished personality.

Leaders need to develop competencies in five teaching areas:

1. Generate compelling interest around a new competency

Educators need to be able to create an interest and curiosity for the learner. This will motivate the learner to participate in active learning. They will put their complete efforts into learning a new competency with more dedication and interest. The educator just needs to ignite the fire of interest, rest will all fall in place.

2. Develop a learning partnership

Educators need to take the action plan to work shoulder to shoulder with their learners. Educators need to be a cold learner with the learner group they deal with. This makes the learners feel oneness and they will be able to share their ideas and understanding of the new competencies boldly.

3. Encourage deep understanding

Educators need to allow the learner to understand the basic foundation of the new skill, the reason behind the competency, and the rationale for the change. This will enable a deep understanding of the concept and will transform to the application of the concept as well.

4. Facilitate critical unlearning

Learners need guidance on what we need to be forgotten, what needs to be left behind, and what needs to be ignored as they move forward. The educator should be able to facilitate critical unlearning which makes learners learn the new competencies in a better way.

5. Illuminate the entire learning pathway

Learning about one individual concept or skill will not be enough. It will not complete the teaching-learning process. Learning is complete only when the learner understands the function and process of a whole level. Great leader educators can bring that pathway to life for the learners in their classroom. This will illuminate the entire learning pathway.

The primary focus of leadership should be to **identify, grow and support** to enhance the education system and positively impact students learning. Educator-leaders collectively work to improve quality education. They are not only cultivated by individual learners but built and supported by the whole system. Educators can improve themselves when they are connected to support that helps them learn. They become leaders when their ideas build in confidence and support learners.

Foundational concepts of effective leadership

Leaders and titles are not mutually inclusive

An individual can lead forward from anywhere. The title is not necessary. Simply holding the title will not solve the issue. One shouldn't stay back as they don't have a position to lead. Holding a leadership position does not instantly make us into good leaders.

Courageous key

Leadership is the most observed and least understood phenomenon on Earth. Courage is not a physical image; it is the mental ability to handle a situation wisely. Leaders need to be authentic, communicative, confident, inspirational, and lastly courageous. With courage, one can achieve authenticity, communication, confidence, and inspiration. Authentic leaders can establish long-term and meaningful relationships that lead to results.

Leadership is not as complex

Many people have the misconception that leadership lies in making tough decisions. But the decisions that are relevant to a situation are obvious. A leader needs to make decisions based on what is right, but not what is easy, what makes happy, feels good, or any other constraints. It is not difficult to know what action needs to be taken. The complexity lies in making the right decision.

Leaders are made every day by the choices and decisions we make. Ignore the fear and let courage guide our path of actions.

Checklist for being Leader-Educator:

- Being consistent and authentic
- communicate in expectations
- Providing support

- Imbibing the vision
- Maintaining the standard

Amazing Fact !!!

What is simultaneously thrilling and terrifying about being an educator?

It is that you can have a profound and memorable effect on learners, with an action that educators may have no memory of. So, lead simply and courageously from where you are, and the difference you make in the lives of learners will be lasting powerful, and memorable.

Educators as Nation Builders

Educators are considered as the future builders of our country. They are the providers of knowledge and wisdom to the younger generations. They are the face of educational institutions. They are the only source of education for almost all the people of the country and they are the ones who build the future of the nation.

The educators have the power to decide what the nation has to look like and educate the learners accordingly. They have the strength and the ability to fight for a prosperous country and make India a powerful and well-educated nation.

Undoubtedly, educators play a vital role in nation-building because the future exists in their hands. They are the fortune builders of the country. We cannot imagine a country without educators. Without them, it will only be a country of utter chaos. There will be hardly anybody to take initiative and make sure the children get quality education and the knowledge required to lead a pious and healthy life. There will be no progress in the country without education.

Below mentioned are a few characteristics of the roles that our educators play every single day-

Preparing learners for a challenging life –Initiating from a very early age, the educators take the kids away from their parents for a few hours and teach them in a completely different atmosphere. They try and make the environment learning-friendly, but it is still varied from the environment at home. In this process, educators prepare their learners for an environment in which they might have to be upfront in their lives.

Literacy and wisdom – The educators not only teach the learners to impart knowledge, but they also provide words of wisdom every day which shapes the personality and character of the young ones. Many learners are more influenced by their educators than their parents. The educator needs to be selfless and believe in providing wise information to their learners at all times.

A friend, philosopher, and guide – Today's education has adopted a new system of teaching named learner-centered teaching leaving the teacher-centered teaching behind. We find that educators have dissolved the basic image of a strict educator and have become much more for their learners. Educators provide a friendly shoulder to give courage to their learners. Educators provide their learners with life lessons by showing videos and reading books of famous personalities. The educators guide the learner in various aspects and encourage them.

Well-wishers – educators are the well-wishers of their learners. They own their learners and sometimes respond beyond the parents. Educators have complete knowledge of the child as they spend more tin=me in school than at home. Educators always try and bridge the balance between all things and make sure that the child's future isn't affected.

Nation builder – A nation comprises children more than adults. The children are the future of a nation and the educators are the ones who are preparing them for their future. With optimum education, wisdom, exposure, and resources, the educators build the nation for tomorrow, brick by brick with a strong foundation, in the belief that the nation grows in flying colors and reaches heights.

Teaching as a profession is probably the most challenging because it imbibes all the other professions to help a child grow. To be successful, one needs to have good communication skills, managerial skills, reading and writing skills, storytelling skills, and many more. The educators train learners in all aspects.

The educators have selflessly and courageously chosen the path of teaching, where they will always be working for mankind and its good. Not everybody has the heart to do it. The leaders of today are training the leaders of tomorrow.

Educator as Mentor

The act of mentoring is a series of ongoing achievements. Mentoring is training and guiding the learners by building trust and encouraging a positive attitude. An effective mentor understands their role and helps the learners in need. Any individual can become a mentor. One need not be a qualified educator or a subject expert to become a good mentor.

Mentors will be able to make a real impact on their learners through building a relationship. For learners coming from less than ideal circumstances, mentoring can be a critical ingredient for bringing a positive outcome.

Educator teaches the subject in a suitable way adapting various strategies that help learners acquire knowledge. But a mentor teaches both skills and character. Skills are usually taught intentionally. It needs a particular time, place, and prior planning to teach skills. Character enhancement is not taught intentionally. A mentor is an adviser, tutor, role model, master, supporter, and sponsor.

For example, Teaching is like note-making what the educator is speaking or writing on the board, while mentoring is to enlighten the learner to visualize the concept and apply it in the real world.

Who needs to be mentored?

- You should only mentor learners who are ready, willing, and able to grow.
- You can mentor only a Faithful, Available & Teachable learner.

- Effective mentoring requires a customized growth plan that fits the learner.
- Both the mentor and the learner being mentored should be on a personal growth program.

Four-step process of mentoring

Step 1: I do, you watch and learn

Step 2: We do task together

Step 3: You do the task and I give feedback

Step 4: You do the task all by yourself

Characteristics of Mentor

Knowledge

Knowledge is referred to plans, aims, and objectives, specialist knowledge in a specific subject area.

Personal skills

Personal skills refer to motivating, influencing, listening, fact-finding, time-management, counseling. Initially, you may not have all these skills, but in a course of time, one will develop the skills.

Qualities

Open-mindedness, enthusiasm, curiosity, willingness, confidentiality, commitment are the required qualities. These are essential because learners need to trust and discuss their thoughts with the mentor.

Experience

Some situations of mentoring require experience while others don't require it. Credibility like age, common sense, practicality are basic experiences that are valued as a mentor. There are some people who when met give often an aura that is filled with confidence, inspiring and innovation.

Skills need to be developed for mentorship

- Maintain good conduct in dealing with learners
- Genuine interest in enhancing learner abilities
- Self-up-gradation of skills and latest technologies
- Patience and interpersonal skills and ability to work in an unstructured program.
- Can command respect for the learner

Mentor Benefits

Being a mentor benefits educators both personally and professionally. Personally one will be satisfied for being strength to their learners. Professionally, mentoring enables an educator to hold the role of a leader and advisor.

There are a few more benefits of being a mentor:

- Develops leadership and management skills
- Provides a platform to impart knowledge and guidance
- Provides satisfaction and enhances personal growth
- Helps in being self-motivated
- Demonstrates involvement in volunteering

Mentor Competencies

- **Communication:** language and clarity in speech
- **Self-awareness:** Being noticeable about things going around
- **Humor:** Sense of humor promotes solace to the mentored learner
- **Passionate:** Interest in enhancing the character and personality

- **Relationship management:** Maintain a healthy relation
- **Goal clarity:** visualize the goal
- **Conceptual modeling:** Acquire knowledge in the subject

Mentoring Pyramid:

Importance of Professional Development for Educators

Learning — Never-Ending Process

Education is a continuous process. Professional development is life-long learning and growing as an educator. With professional development, educators and academic administrators can always have the potential to upgrade their skills. It helps career-oriented educators to enhance their skills and attain professionalism. It keeps the educator informed and updated about innovations in the teaching platform. By incorporating such techniques in the classroom one can be a successful educator.

Outcomes of Learning

The technology involved in teaching and the standard in curricula are changing continuously. This makes it more challenging for educators to meet up with the latest trends. Professional development makes it possible for educators to become stronger and more fitting to teach the present generation.

Results of research say that the learner achievement increases by twenty-one percentile because of professional development for educators. Having knowledge and experience is alone not enough, as an educator, professionalism in teacher education is highly recommended.

Implementing new teaching techniques

Acquiring knowledge in professional development classes like; seminars, workshops, symposiums, and faculty development classes, educators try to implement the new techniques in their classrooms and teaching style. They also introduce new methods of assessment styles, maintaining records, lesson planning, and effective presentation which upgrade the educator in a wholesome way.

Organizing and Management

An educator's time is mostly spent on classroom teaching, evaluating learners' work, and other deskwork. Professional training for educators helps them to plan time efficiently and stay organized in their works. This makes their work more effective, efficient, and presentable.

Knowledge Acquisition

Learners expect their educators to be subject experts. Professional development makes sure that educators answer every question the learner poses in the class. Professional development enables educators to acquire knowledge in various aspects of the subject. Professional development not only gives knowledge about classroom management, administration, and evaluation, it also helps in acquiring knowledge in subject matters.

Source of Support and Motivation

Attending professional development courses gives educators a chance to step out of their regular schedule. Educators get to meet other educators from different areas and exchange their ideas about classroom teaching. It gives the educators support and motivation to modify themselves as better educator.

Professional development is nurturing the skills of the educators to handle the teaching and administration responsibilities effectively. Educators become future leaders with the assistance of professional development courses.

Professional Goals

Professional development and goal settings will go side by side. Educators need to set up professional goals. The time invested in seminars and workshops looks hard to schedule, but the results of attending such courses are immeasurable.

The goals set should be SMART—Smart, Measurable, Attainable, Relevant, and Time bounded. Setting up career goals needs to be clear, realistic, and achievable. They should involve a purpose and be time-bound to achieve it. This makes the educator unique.

Plan, Prepare, Action and Feedback are the goals for achieving success in the classroom.

Professional education implementation has numerous advantages both for learners and educators. It helps to enhance the skills and make better educators and thus grow into good administrators. It makes the class a 'learning paradise'.

An Eye-Opener

After a long observation of a teacher training class, the educator said to one of the meritorious trainees that "you are not yet ready to be a mentor teacher and you need to be a learner always". The trainee was not happy with the statement and expressed that as she is the topper of the class, she needs nothing to learn more. She also said that she could be the best teacher.

Hearing the trainee's words, the educator gave the trainee a task. She was given a month to teach a potter who makes and sells pots beside the college. She was also handed over the material that has to be taught. The trainee accepted it happily as it was pretty easy for her to teach, being a trained and meritorious teacher trainee.

Days passed by and the day arrived when the trainee was called upon by the educator. The trainee appeared in front of the educator with a long disappointed face. She admitted that she wasn't ready yet and needs something more to learn. When the educator inquired about the reason, the trainee said, I visited the potter every day and was sincere in my preparation to teach. But, he was so busy that he had no time for learning.

The educator smiled and asked the trainee, in your regular visits to the potter, have you learned anything from him? The trainee asked the educator what would I learn from the potter? The educator then explained that as you visited his place regularly for a month, you must have learned the basics of making a pot or the way he deals with people to sell his pots.

An educator must be an all-time learner. Be it in any situation, be it from anyone, the urge to learn must never be suppressed. Learning is the striking tool for a teacher's success. It helps to keep up on par with the changes in society, the latest trends, and technology.

'Without up-gradation, one will become a vintage piece'

Awards – Token of Appreciation

Recognizing the efforts of an individual, in building up certain work in any given field, by a token of appreciation is regarded as an award. In various fields, awards are given to individuals for their outstanding performance and innovative work. Individuals don't work for awards, but their creativity, hard work, and dedication towards their work, which help a group of people and make their lives easy, bring them recognition in the form of an award.

Awards are not only given to successful people; many other qualities are recognized like a struggle, ability, effort, authenticity, help or useful for at least a group of people, and above all excellence. Very few remarkable individuals win fame and encouragement to pursue their excellent work through various awards.

As in other fields, awards are given in education platforms for teaching and administration heads; educators, and principals. Educator awards are given at the national and international levels.

National Awards

The **'National Award to Teachers'** is awarded by the Indian Government to educators every academic year. It is awarded by the President of India to give public recognition to meritorious educators working in primary, middle, and secondary schools in India. The purpose of this award is to celebrate the unique contribution of some of the finest teachers in the country and to honor them for their commitment to this field which not only improved the quality of school education but also enriched the lives of their learners. The award is awarded to the educators annually on the 5th of September, which is celebrated as National Teacher's Day, in memory of Sri. Sarvepalli Radhakrishnan.

Similarly, every state government of India also celebrates the contribution of educators to the field and honors them with the **'Best Teacher Award'** and **'Best Principal Award'** annually on the 5th of September, which is celebrated as National Teacher's Day. It is awarded by the Governor of the state to give public recognition to meritorious educators working in primary, middle, and secondary schools in the states of India.

There are many private organizations, which honor the educators of private schools for their immense work, incredible talent and for extending their service in favor of the learners.

International Awards

The **'Global Teaching Excellence Awards (GTEA)'** is organized to identify, invite, concede and implement changes in the education sector's individuals & organizations working appreciably to pioneer & revolutionize the Education system. It is a token of appreciation towards illustrious minds for their impeccable contribution to the education sector. International Education Awards accredits educators who have helped learners to reach their goals by equipping them with opportunities and resources in exploring knowledge.

The **'Global Teacher Prize'** is referred to by journalists as the 'Noble Prize for teaching'. A US$1 million award by the Varkey Foundation is awarded to the educator who has made an outstanding contribution to the teaching profession. Nominations of educators, meeting the mentioned criteria are open to the worldwide public, and educators nominate themselves. The judging is done by the

Global Teacher Prize Academy, consisting of head teachers, education experts, commentators, journalists, public officials, tech entrepreneurs, company directors, and scientists from around the world.

The AKS Education Awards are one of the most prestigious awards. They honor excellent educators from all over the World with the **'Global Teacher Award (GTA)'**. It is awarded to the educators extending their contribution in community building and helping make a better society through their inspirational teaching.

The AKS Education Awards offers the **'Global Faculty Award (GFA)'** by actively reaching out to all corners of the world to identify, recognize exceptional teaching faculty who has made an outstanding contribution to their profession, demonstrated excellence in teaching different subjects, shown outstanding contribution to learners and served the community through real-life teaching.

Why is Change Needed?

This is the story of an EAGLE

'The King of the Sky'

Eagle usually has a life span of 70 years.

But, to live long, it needs to take a tough decision in its 40th year.

At the age of 40,

Its long flexible talons can no longer grab prey which servers as its food,

Its long sharp beak bends.

The feathers become old, thick, and heavy not permitting it to fly high

The thick feathers stick to its chest and make it impossible to fly

Then, the eagle is left with two options:

DIE or go through the painful process of **CHANGE**.

This process requires the eagle to rest at the mountain top.

Then the eagle knocks its beak against a rock until it plucks out and waits patiently for the new beak to grow.

With the new beak, it plucks the talons when the new talons grow,

It starts plucking its old, thick, and heavy feathers.

CHANGE that worth sustaining pain

And after this …..

The eagle takes its flight high in the sky

The king is back

And it continues its life journey for another 30 years

Why is change needed?

To survive,

We too have to start the process of change

Unlike the eagle, we need to pluck our unpleasant memories and fixed mindset

And take the advantage of the present.

To take a new journey ahead in the future, let go of the negative old limiting beliefs

Open up your fixed mindset and

Let yourself fly again like an EAGLE.

Things to learn from this **KINGLY BIRD**

➢ **Don't be a parrot life**

A parrot talks too much but cannot fly high. But, an eagle is silent and has the willpower to touch the sky. 'Live life **KING SIZE**'.

➢ **Eagles fly alone**

Eagles don't fly with other small birds, which tell stay away from narrow-minded people who pull you down. There is a saying your friends determine the personality and character you possess which means maintain good company, as eagles fly only with eagles.

➢ **Eagles have Vision**

They can focus on something that is at 5Km away, No matter whatever the hurdles, it will not move its focus from the prey. This means to have a vision and remain focused in life. No matter what the challenges you come across, don't give up and you will succeed.

➢ **Eagles are fearless**

They do not surrender themselves to the size or strength of their prey. They will always fight to win their territory. Meaning successful people don't give up. They fight without fear.

➢ **Eagles are Tenacious**

Eagles love storms. They get excited with the clouds gathering. They use the raging storm winds and lift themselves higher above the clouds. This enables the eagle opportunity to glide and rest its wings. Meaning achievers are not afraid of challenges. They relish them and use them for their profitability.

- **Eagles don't savage**
  They eat the prey they hunt. They do not eat dead meat. This means we should look for new frontiers and challenges to conquer but not depend on our past success.

- **Prepare for training**
  They remove the feathers in the soft grass of the nest so that the young ones get uncomfortable in preparation for flying and eventually their fly becomes unbearable to stay in the nest. Meaning leave your comfort zone, there is no growth there.

Bibliography

Books

- Kay, D. and Hinds,R (2009) A practical guide to mentoring, Howtobooks,Oxford
- Cole, M and Cole, S (1989). The Development of Children, Scientific American Books, New York
- Mishra, A (2007), Everyday Life in a Slum in Delhi. In D.K. Behera (Ed.) Childhood in South Asia. New Delhi: Pearson Education India
- Bhatt, H. The diary of a school teacher: An Azim Premji University publications, www.arvindguptatoys.com/arvindgupta/diary - school teacher- eng.pdf
- Burden, Paul R; Byrd, David. M. (1999). Methods for Effective Teaching (Sec Edition), Allyn and Bacon.
- Carr, D (2005), Making Sense of Education: An Introduction to the Philosophy and Theory of Education and Teaching, Routledge.
- Kumar Krishna (1997). What is Worth Teaching, Orient Longman, New Delhi.
- Margaret, K.T. The open Classroom, Orient Longman: New Delhi, 1999.
- Julka, A.(2015) Including Children with Special Needs: Upper Primary Stage, NCERT, New Delhi.
- Anice James,(2005),Teaching of Mathematics, Neelkamal Publications Pvt. Ltd. , Hyderabad,India
- The Right of Children to Free and Compulsory Education Act-2009, The Gazette of India, 2009

- Chomsky (1964) in Day. E. M (2002): Identity and the young English language learner; Multilingual Matters Limited; London.
- Kay Burke (2006) From Standards to Rubrics in 6 Steps, Tools for Assessing Student Learning, K-8, Corwing Press, A Sage Publicaitons Company, California.
- Singh H.S. (1974) Modern Educational Testing. New Delhi: Sterling Publication
- Ahmad, J., Ahmad, M.S. and Khan, A. (2012), Computer Applications in Education, Neelkamal Publication, Hyderabad, PP-288, ISBN: 978-81-8316-293-7.
- Dalal, A.S. (ed) (2001). A Greater Psychology – An Introduction to the Psychological thoughts of Sri Aurobindo. Puducherry, Sri Aurobindo Ashram
- Bhatt, H. The diary of a school teacher. An Azim Premji University Publication. Retrieved from www.arvindguptatoys.com/arvindgupta/diary-school-teachereng.pdf
- Mukunda, K.V. (2009). What did you ask at school today? A handbook of child learning, Harper Collins
- Pegg.M (2006)The Art of Mentoring Management Books 2000
- Clutterbuck.D (2004) Everyone needs a mentor, foruth edition London,CIPD
- How to ask right questions by Patrica Blosser
- Discursive approaches to research in mathematics education by Carolyn Kieran, Ellice Forman, and Anna Sfard.
- Inclusive Education for Children with Special Needs— by Neena Dash

- **Uncommon Sense Teaching— Book by Barbara Oakley, Beth Rogowsky, and Terry Sejnowski**
- Your Students, My Students, Our Students: Rethinking Equitable and Inclusive Classrooms—by Julie Kroener, Lee Ann Jung, Douglas B. Fisher, Nancy Frey
- Take Control of the Noisy Class: Chaos to Calm in 15 Seconds (Super-effective classroom management strategies for teachers in today's toughest classrooms) by Rob Plevin
- Classroom Management by Mangla A. B.

Websites:
- https://education.stateuniversity.com/pages/1916/Discourse.html
- https://learningdiscourses.com/
- https://www.uopeople.edu/blog/what-is-the-multiple-intelligences-theory/
- https://www.indianyouth.net/role-of-teachers-in-nation-building/
- https://www.educationdegree.com/articles/25-ways-teachers-can-be-role-models/
- https://online.queens.edu/resources/article/professional-development-for-educators/
- https://www.meraevents.com/blog/importance-of-professional-development-for-teachers
- https://resumes-for-teachers.com/blog/professional-development/what-is-the-importance-of-teacher-professional-development/
- https://www.prodigygame.com/in-en/blog/teacher-professional-development/
- https://learningforward.org/wp-content/uploads/2017/08/professional-development-matters.pdf

- https://teachersbadi.in/ap-national-awards-teachers-online-application-form-apply-online-cseap/
- https://teachersbadi.in/national-best-techers-awards-best-teachers-selected-list-national-awards/
- https://nationalawardstoteachers.education.gov.in/Guidelines.aspx
- https://aksawards.com/gta/AboutUs
- https://www.globalteacherprize.org/
- https://nationalawardstoteachers.education.gov.in/
- http://gteaglobal.com/
- https://gfa.aksawards.com/
- https://www.youtube.com/watch?v=h8_T40WKSsw
- https://www.youtube.com/hashtag/ctetexpert
- https://www.youtube.com/watch?v=N2D_oEJ1KYs

www.ingramcontent.com/pod-product-compliance
Ingram Content Group UK Ltd.
Pitfield, Milton Keynes, MK11 3LW, UK
UKHW042001230426
12048UKWH00009B/471